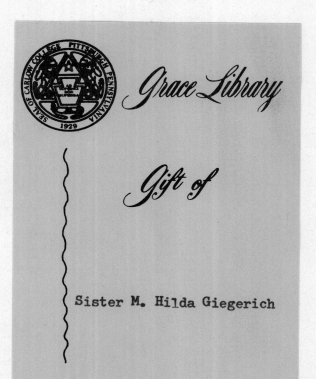

FRA ANGELICO
by
John Pope-Hennessy

PHAIDON

THE ANNUNCIATORY ANGEL. Detail from the fresco of the Annunciation at San Marco, Florence.

FRA ANGELICO

BY

JOHN POPE-HENNESSY

PHAIDON PUBLISHERS INC

DISTRIBUTED BY GARDEN CITY BOOKS NEW YORK

PREFACE

THE work of Fra Angelico presents one of the most difficult interpretative problems of fifteenth-century Italian painting. In the present book practically all the paintings ascribed to Fra Angelico are reproduced, but the catalogue of autograph works illustrated in the plates is more restricted than in any previous monograph. In this connection I should make it clear that paintings have been excluded from the catalogue only where prolonged examination has convinced me that they cannot logically be retained. I have studied in the original all the paintings illustrated in the plates, with the exception of those in the Des Cars collection and at Leningrad, Houston and Harvard, and all the paintings discussed in the appendix save those marked with an asterisk. A few paintings of low quality, or not closely connected with Angelico, have been omitted from the book. As a result of this reduction of the artist's work, it has been possible to isolate, from the mass of paintings traditionally ascribed to Fra Angelico, a group of masterpieces in which the workings of an individual artistic personality can be discerned. Many of the standard photographs of the artist's paintings give at best a misleading impression of the originals, and I am obliged to my publishers, to Professor Filippo Rossi of the Soprintendenza alle Gallerie at Florence and to Professor D. R. de Campos of the Musei Pontifici for authorizing the making of new photographs. I am also indebted for photographic material to the Casa Editrice Electa. One of the main obstacles to an understanding of Angelico is the condition of his paintings, which have been more ruthlessly restored than those of any other Florentine Renaissance artist. In a few plates I have preferred to reproduce old photographs, which show the paintings before retouching deprived them of their expressiveness.

1952   JOHN POPE-HENNESSY

CONTENTS

INTRODUCTION

FRA ANGELICO is one of the most familiar of Italian artists. In his own lifetime churches and cathedrals competed for his work, and the idiom he evolved has come to be regarded as the natural language of religious painting. For more than a century the popular image of an angel has been that of an angel by Angelico.

In literature, Angelico the maker of religious pictographs has assumed precedence over Angelico the artist. Soon after his death he figures in the *De Vita et Obitu B. Mariae* of the Dominican, Domenico da Corella, as 'Angelicus pictor . . . Iohannes nomine, non Jotto, non Cimabove minor', and later in the century he is mentioned in a celebrated rhymed poem by Giovanni Santi between Gentile da Fabriano and Pisanello, and alongside Fra Filippo Lippi, Pesellino and Domenico Veneziano, as 'Giovan da Fiesole frate al bene ardente'. But with the advent of Savonarola, for whom art was a means of spiritual propaganda, there developed a new attitude towards painting; and after Savonarola's heroic death, Angelico, the friar artist, was adopted by his followers as the pivot round which these theories could revolve. Already in the first narrative account of the artist's life, a brief biography included in a volume of Dominican eulogies published by Leandro Alberti in 1517, is implicit the case that was formulated in the nineteenth century: that Angelico's superior stature as an artist was due to his superior stature as a man. Alberti's eulogy was one of the sources drawn on by Vasari when in 1550 he printed the first formal life of Fra Angelico. Another source was a Dominican friar, Fra Eustachio, who had received the habit from Savonarola, and who, as a man of almost eighty, transmitted to Vasari the conventual legends woven round the artists of San Marco. A fellow-Dominican, Timoteo Bottonio, tells us how Vasari 'used often to come to gossip with this old man, from whom he obtained many beautiful details about these old and illustrious artists'. From these and other sources Vasari built up his life. 'Fra Giovanni,' he writes, 'was a simple man and most holy in his habits. . . . He was most gentle and temperate, living chastely, removed from the cares of the world. He would often say that whoever practised art needed a quiet life and freedom from care, and that he who occupied himself with the things of Christ ought always to be with Christ. . . . I cannot bestow too much praise on this holy father, who was so humble and modest in all his works and conversation, so fluent and devout in his painting, the saints by his hand being more like those blessed beings than those of any other. He never retouched or repaired any of his pictures, always leaving them in the condition in which they were first seen, believing, so he said, that this was the will of God. Some say that Fra Giovanni never took up his brush without first making a prayer. He never made a Crucifix when the tears did not course down his cheeks, while the goodness of his sincere and great soul in religion may be seen from the attitudes of his figures.' On one point alone did Vasari allow himself the luxury of scepticism: 'He was never seen in anger among the friars, which seems to me an extraordinary thing and almost impossible to believe; his habit was to smile and reprove his friends.' In the mouth of nineteenth-century commentators Vasari's words take on a romantic overtone. 'On peut dire de lui,' runs a celebrated passage in Rio's *De l'Art Chrétien*, 'que la peinture n'était autre chose que sa formule favorite pour les actes de foi, d'espérance et d'amour; pour que sa tâche ne fût pas indigne de celui en vue duquel il l'entreprenait, jamais il ne mettait la main à l'œuvre sans avoir imploré la bénédiction du ciel, et quand la voix intérieure lui disait que sa prière avait été exaucée, il ne se croyait plus en droit de rien changer au produit de l'inspiration qui lui était venue d'en haut, persuadé qu'en cela comme dans tout le reste il n'était que l'instrument de la volonté de Dieu. Toutes les fois qu'il peignait Jésus-Christ sur la croix, les larmes lui coulaient des yeux avec autant d'abondance que s'il eût assisté à cette dernière scène de la passion sur le Calvaire.'

This reliance upon inspiration, these empathetic tears, these acts of faith have been recounted by many writers since the time of Rio. But though they still fulfil the purpose for which they were designed, that of commending the artist's work to simple-minded people in search of spiritual nourishment, they form an obstacle to any understanding of Angelico. A simple amateur guided by faith? Yet the author of these paintings is uncompromisingly professional. A mystic at the mercy of chance inspiration? Yet his schemes have the appearance of resulting from close thought and of having been subjected to scrupulous analysis. Where there is so sharp an antithesis between written tradition and pictorial style, it is on the evidence of the works of art that our verdict must be based, and these show Angelico to have been a painter of great formal inventiveness and of the utmost sensibility, whose work was the expression not so much of his own mystical experience as of a trend in the religious thinking of his time.

For the little that we know of Angelico's origins we are indebted to a sentence in the sixteenth-century chronicle of San Domenico at Fiesole, which tells us that in 1407 'Fr. Joannes Petri de Mugello iuxta Vichium, optimus pictor, qui multas tabulas et parietes in diversis locis pinxit, accepit habitum clericorum in hoc conventu . . . et in sequenti anno fecit professionem.' According to Vasari, his Christian name was Guido, and he was born in 1387. He was thus aged twenty when he received the habit of the Dominican Order at Fiesole, and twenty-one when he made his profession in 1408. His brother (younger than the painter if Vasari is to be believed, older according to some modern critics) entered the order at the same time under the name of Benedetto, and took his solemn vows.

The Dominican rule, like the rules of other religious orders, was open to a number of different interpretations. In the last years of the fourteenth century the tendency towards reform, that is towards a stricter and more literal interpretation of its provisions, had taken shape in the movement known as the Dominican Observance. The originator of the Observant movement was Raymond of Capua, the confessor of St Catherine of Siena, and its protagonist was his disciple, the preacher Giovanni Dominici. With the return of Dominici to Central Italy from his apostolate in Venice, the vogue of the Observant movement spread, and the number of recruits whom it attracted became greater than the reformed houses at Città di Castello and Cortona could absorb. In 1405 the Dominican Bishop of Fiesole made available to the observants a vineyard beneath the town, and here there rose the new foundation of San Domenico. A year later, with thirteen companions, Dominici took possession of the convent. Angelico may have had no direct contact with Dominici, for in 1407 the great preceptor had already left Fiesole for Rome, and from 1409, when he was appointed Cardinal, until his death ten years later he was engaged mainly on matters of church policy. But his teachings, perpetuated in the *Lucula Noctis* and the *Trattato della santa carità*, determined the intellectual climate of San Domenico, and through them and through two of his disciples, Sant'Antonino (who had joined the Order in 1405) and the Blessed Lorenzo of Ripafratta (then in charge of the Observant novitiate at Cortona, where Angelico must have joined Sant'Antonino soon after his reception at Fiesole), he exercised an oblique influence over Angelico's development.

Dominici's most important work, the *Lucula Noctis*, is a defence of traditional spirituality against the onslaughts of the humanists. Let the Christian cultivate the earth rather than study heathen books; let him read not the poetry of antiquity but 'the Holy Writ, in which the Lord has laid out the true poetry of wisdom, and the true eloquence of the spirit of truth'. Let those who have charge of the young remember that 'Christ is our only guide to happiness . . . our father, our leader, our light, our food, our redemption, our way, our truth, our life'; let them recall that 'as the years of tender youth flow by, the soft wax may take on any form. Stamp on it the impress not of Narcissus, Myrrha, Phaedra or Ganymede, but of the crucified Christ and of the Saints'. Let them, above all, propagate the faith, through which the Christian is permitted year by year to warm his frozen mind before the crib. Two aspects of Dominici's thought are of special importance for an understanding of the paintings of Angelico. The first is his fear of rhetoric. 'The beautiful form of the poem,' he writes, 'is like clothing. The body is worth more than the clothes which cover it, and the soul worth more than both.' The second is his rejection of personal revelation, that concomitant of mysticism. Whereas Savonarola, with his belief in the validity of individual visions, inculcated a personal religious imagery in the artists he inspired, the painting produced under the aegis of Dominici was the expression of collective, and not of individual, mystical experience.

In the absence of indications to the contrary, Angelico is assumed to have shared the vicissitudes which overtook his brethren in 1409, when the Synod of Pisa elected the anti-pope Alexander V. Supported by a strong party in Tuscany, Alexander V and his successor John XXIII reckoned among their adherents the Master-General of the Dominican Order and the Bishop of Fiesole. The Observant Dominicans, on the other hand, owing partly to the personal devotion of Dominici to Gregory XII, remained loyal to the Pope. After their Prior had been arrested on

1. VIRGIN AND CHILD ENTHRONED WITH EIGHT ANGELS BETWEEN SAINTS THOMAS AQUINAS, BARNABAS, DOMINIC AND PETER MARTYR. San Domenico, Fiesole. *Below:* THE RISEN CHRIST ADORED BY SAINTS AND ANGELS. National Gallery, London.

instructions from the Master-General, they left their convent and fled to Foligno, where they were joined two years later by the community from San Domenico at Cortona, when this town came under the authority of Florence and Pope John XXIII. At Foligno they remained until 1414, when the plague forced them to move back to Cortona. Four years later, after unity had been established with the election of Martin V to the papacy, their convent at Fiesole was restored to them.

In a letter addressed to the nuns of the reformed convent of Corpus Christi in Venice, Dominici extols the painting of illuminated manuscripts as a discipline conducive to pure and holy thoughts. Both from his correspondence and from the letters of the Pisan mystic, the Beata Chiara Gamba-corti, it appears that miniature illumination was extensively practised in reformed Dominican communities. Angelico's brother, Fra Benedetto, is known to have been active as a scribe, and was perhaps also an illuminator. If Angelico painted miniatures, all trace of them has disappeared, and it is not even certain that in these early years he practised as an artist. But once back in Fiesole, he must have begun or resumed painting, for about 1428 he executed his first surviving work, an altarpiece for the high altar of San Domenico (Fig. 1; Pls. 3–7).

In 1418, when the Observant community returned, the church and convent were re-endowed under the will of a rich merchant, Barnaba degli Agli, and in 1435 they were re-dedicated to his patron saint, St Barnabas. This saint appears beside the Virgin and Child in Angelico's painting. About 1500 the altarpiece was modernized, and when we visit the church of San Domenico to-day we find a rectangular panel, in which the figures are set before a distant landscape seen through the arches of a classical arcade. Fortunately the form of the original panels can still be discerned, and it is clear that the painting was planned as a triptych, and that the Saints were shown on a gold ground. The predella, a *Risen Christ adored by Saints and Angels* now in the National Gallery, London (Fig. 1, Pls. 6, 7), was retained when the altarpiece was modified, but new pilasters were adapted from another painting. Two of the ten original pilaster panels, conforming closely to the style of the main panels of the altarpiece, are in the Musée Condé at Chantilly (Fig. II). The loose grouping and cursive drawing of the angels in the centre of the altarpiece seem to support the view that initially Angelico was trained as an illuminator. But the forms differ from those employed in the best-known miniaturist studio of the time, the Camaldo-lese school of book illumination directed at Santa Maria degli Angeli by Lorenzo Monaco, and Angelico's master may have been some Dominican illuminator, perhaps the artist who, in 1417, prepared a number of graphic illustrations of the journey of the Dominican Fra Pietro della Croce to the Holy Land (Fig. XLIX). An attempt has been made to identify these drawings as the earliest known works of Angelico. In the predella only the two outer panels, with effigies of Dominican saints and beati, are by the same hand as the main panels of the altarpiece, and the three inner panels are by another hand. The presence of a collaborator in this painting serves to remind us that Angelico almost certainly emerged from a conventual miniaturist workshop, and that the medieval ideals of this workshop were carried through into the co-operative and self-effacing practice of his own studio.

If we seek a point of reference for the style of the polyptych at San Domenico, we find it in an altarpiece painted by Masolino for Santa Maria Maggiore in Florence about 1428. Comparing the central groups in the two paintings, with their soft lines and their rich modelling, or the St Julian of Masolino with Angelico's St Peter Martyr, it becomes clear that the two pictures are couched in the same idiom, and can have been separated by no more than a few years. The probability, therefore, is that the San Domenico polyptych was painted not, as is frequently assumed, about 1418, but after 1425. The relationship between the artists is less easy to define than the relationship between their paintings. Four years older than Angelico, Masolino had been trained in the worshop of Ghiberti, and in 1425 was engaged, with his disciple Masaccio, in decorating the Brancacci Chapel. It is possible that in 1418, when his community returned to

San Domenico, Angelico, at the advanced age of thirty, served his apprenticeship in Masolino's studio. More probably the Masolinesque phase represented by the San Domenico polyptych resulted from some gradual process of assimilation, through which Angelico moved by degrees towards Masolino and away from some earlier, more archaic style. After Masaccio's death in 1428 the two painters bifurcate; whereas in Masolino Gothic elements tend to reassert themselves, in Angelico they are progressively reduced, until in the mid-thirties the Gothic structure of his polyptychs is at variance with his treatment of the human form. How strong were these anti-Gothic proclivities may be judged from a *Madonna* in the Museo di San Marco (Fig. 2), which must have been executed not long after the altarpiece in San Domenico, and is based on the central panel of a polyptych painted by Lorenzo Monaco for Monte Oliveto in 1406–10. Here almost all of the characteristically Gothic features of Lorenzo Monaco's design are abandoned or modified, and the figures are invested with a classical simplicity.

The San Domenico polyptych was not the only work painted by Angelico for the convent at Fiesole. A tabernacle on the high altar,

2. VIRGIN AND CHILD ENTHRONED. Museo di San Marco, Florence.

presumably undertaken at the same time as the polyptych, is noted by Vasari. More important are three frescoes, one of which, a *Christ on the Cross* (Pl. 1), remains in the Sala Capitolare of the convent, while the others, a *Virgin and Child with Saints Dominic and Thomas Aquinas* (Fig. 3) and a *Christ on the Cross adored by Saint Dominic with the Virgin and Saint John* (Fig. 4), formerly in the refectory, are now in Leningrad and Paris. In the history of conventual decoration these paintings mark a new departure in idiom and iconography. The frescoes at Leningrad and Paris, and above all that still at Fiesole, represent an art free from distraction and devoid of decorative accidentals, in which the image, reduced to its simplest terms

3. VIRGIN AND CHILD WITH SAINTS DOMINIC AND THOMAS AQUINAS. Hermitage, Leningrad. (The fresco is shown prior to its removal from San Domenico, Fiesole.)

4. CHRIST ON THE CROSS ADORED BY SAINT DOMINIC
WITH THE VIRGIN AND SAINT JOHN. Louvre, Paris. (The fresco is
shown prior to its removal from San Domenico, Fiesole.)

and presented with the minimum of incident, is designed to be filled out by the religious imagination of the onlooker. In two of them the spectator, in the person of the founder of his Order, participates in the holy scene. These features, consummated in the great frescoes which Angelico painted at San Marco after 1438, are the first fruits of an effort to evolve an art which, in conformity with the teachings of Dominici, might influence the community's spiritual life. As a work of art the *Christ on the Cross* in the Sala Capitolare greatly exceeds in interest the other frescoes from Fiesole, and was probably painted about 1430, some years before these scenes. In Masaccio's *Trinity* in Santa Maria Novella the subject of the crucified Christ had given rise to the noblest composition of the early fifteenth century. The fresco at Fiesole seems to depend directly from this work, for here Angelico, like Masaccio before him, explores the geometrical relationship between the vertical and horizontal of the Cross and the containing arch. But at Fiesole the spatial implications of Masaccio's composition are ignored, and Masaccio's impassive image of the hero on the Cross is replaced by a pathetic portrayal of Christ as crucified man.

Among the lost works of Masaccio recorded by Vasari is an *Annunciation* painted for San Niccolò oltr'Arno, representing 'a house full of columns drawn in perspective of singular beauty . . . in which he showed his thorough understanding of perspective'. Possibly this altarpiece served as the prototype for another early painting by Angelico, the *Annunciation* painted for the church of San Domenico at Cortona, where the artist had spent so many years. Produced soon after 1430, the *Annunciation* at Cortona (Pls. 8–15) is Angelico's first indubitable masterpiece. The scene is set beneath a loggia, closed on two sides by Brunelleschan columns and at the back by an arcaded wall. On the right the Virgin, her hands crossed on her breast, leans forward from her gold-brocaded seat, reciting the words of St Luke inscribed in gold letters on the surface of the panel: 'Behold the handmaid of the Lord; be it unto me according to thy word.' Confronting her with a half-genuflection is the angel, his forefinger raised in expostulation as his lips recite the sentence: 'The Holy Ghost shall come upon thee, and the power of the Highest shall overshadow thee.' Just as the altarpiece of the *Annunciation* painted by Simone Martini in 1333 dictated the treatment of this scene in Siena for more than half a century, so the Cortona altarpiece, with its pervasive sense of mystery, its infectious earnestness, formed the source of countless adaptations and variants. A lost altarpiece painted by Angelico himself in 1432 for the convent of Sant' Alessandro at Brescia may have been a repetition of this scheme. The surviving copies – one of these is at Montecarlo (Fig. v), another from San Domenico at Fiesole is in Madrid (Fig. vi) – lack not only the expressiveness, but the formal distinction of the Cortona altarpiece. In none of them do we find an instinctive sense of volume like that with which the angel's head is realized. In none of them do we find inventions comparable to that by which the long curve of the angel's wings protrudes beyond the colonnade. In none of them do we find, in the garden outside the portico, so radiant a vision of the natural world, or colour of such immaculate translucency.

Barnaba degli Agli, the benefactor of San Domenico, was a member of the Arte della Calimala, and for many years the guild of cloth merchants was closely connected with the convent. A by-product of this connection was the commissioning on 2 July 1433 of a triptych for the guild-hall of the associated Arte dei Linaiuoli or guild of flax-workers. By the terms of his contract, Angelico's triptych was to be painted 'inside and out with gold, blue and silver of the best and finest that can be found', at a cost of 'one hundred and ninety gold florins for the whole and for his craftsman-ship, or for as much less as his conscience shall deem it right to charge'. The Linaiuoli triptych (Pls. 16–24) is the only painting by Angelico commissioned by a secular body, and the concluding clause (for which contracts with lay artists offer no parallel) is explained by the adherence of the Dominican Observance to the principle of individual poverty. One of Angelico's earliest bio-graphers, Manetti, confirms that he 'did not ever paint for money', and declares that 'if payment were made for any work, this was to his convent'. The triptych was intended to occupy a taber-nacle designed by Ghiberti in 1432, and its suitability for this position seems to have been deter-mined from a drawing submitted by Angelico. Five weeks after the contract was concluded, on 11 August 1433, two assistants of Ghiberti, Jacopo di Bartolommeo da Settignano and Simone di Nanni da Fiesole, began work on this marble frame. The frame, with its arched central aperture, conditioned the form of the painting, which consists of a central panel of the Virgin and Child enthroned between two mobile wings. On the inside of the wings (and therefore visible only when the triptych was open) are figures of the two Saints John; on the outside (and therefore visible only when the triptych was closed) are Saints Peter and Mark, scenes from whose legends are illustrated in the predella beneath.

The scale of the Saints in the wings of the Linaiuoli triptych is larger than in the *Annunciation* at Cortona, but they reveal the same unerring instinct for the placing of figures in the picture space. Nowhere in Masolino do we encounter forms so perfectly adapted to the area they fill; and in this again it can be claimed that Angelico had learned the lesson of Masaccio's *Trinity*. The four saints are shown standing on a rocky platform which stops short of the front plane of the paint-ing, a device that lends them the maximum three-dimensional solidity. Some of the most signifi-cant achievements of the first generation of Florentine Renaissance artists were the statues of guild patrons on Or San Michele. It is reasonably certain that Angelico, in designing the lateral panels of the Linaiuoli triptych, had these figures in mind, for not only was the framing of the tabernacle closely similar to those which Ghiberti and other artists had designed for the niches of the statues, not only was the artistic problem, within the limits of a different medium, essentially the same, but the panels themselves represented figures which Ghiberti, Nanni di Banco and Donatello had invested individually with a new character. The sculptor of whose style the four figures are most clearly reminiscent is Nanni di Banco, whom Angelico is said by Vasari to have known well, and the drapery of whose San Severiano shows the same horizontal emphasis as that in the Lin-aiuoli painting. The hieratic figure of the Virgin is surrounded by a wooden frame decorated with twelve music-making angels. By some strange fortuity these have become the most celebrated figures not only of this triptych, but of Angelico's whole œuvre. For the master the least important section of the painting would have been the framework round this panel, and the execution of certain of these little figures seems to have been entrusted to a studio hand. The cartoons of the angels are, however, by Angelico, and form an impressive tribute to his inventiveness.

Beneath the triptych is a predella in three compartments, representing *Saint Peter preaching*

5. THE ADORATION OF THE MAGI. Detail of Plate 16b. Museo di San Marco, Florence.

(Pl. 23), the *Adoration of the Magi* (Fig. 5) and the *Martyrdom of Saint Mark* (Pl. 24). Less attractive than the *Scenes from the Life of the Virgin* beneath the *Annunciation* at Cortona (Pls. 12–15), these scenes bear few traces of the direct observation which the Cortona *Visitation*, with its entrancing view over Lake Trasimene, might lead us to expect. Instead, they are characterized, in the treatment both of the figures and the architecture, by a new solidity, which presupposes knowledge of the Pisa predella of Masaccio. The implications of the designs of the two outer panels become fully apparent when, fifteen years later, elements in them are adapted by Angelico himself for use in the frescoes in the Vatican. Though these panels communicate a sense of the physical reality of the scenes they represent, they are not based on a systematic knowledge of linear perspective. In two somewhat later and more highly organized predellas (one, consisting of an exquisite panel of *The Naming of the Baptist* in the Museo di San Marco and of a scene with *St James freeing Hermogenes* in the Des Cars collection (Pls. 29, 28), from a disassembled polyptych, the other a cycle of *Scenes from the Life of Saint Dominic* (Fig. VIII), painted by a pupil from Angelico's cartoons beneath an altarpiece executed for San Domenico at Cortona about 1436) the method of space representation is still empirical. So far as can be judged it was not till about 1440 that Angelico mastered a technique for depicting bodies in receding space, and to the last this remained more rudimentary than the legitimate construction employed by Uccello and Domenico Veneziano.

The form of the Cortona altarpiece (Pl. 30), a Gothic polyptych with pointed panels, remains faithful to that of the polyptych at Fiesole, and at first sight the painting seems less advanced in style than the Linaiuoli triptych, from which the cartoon of the Virgin enthroned depends. One of the angels beside the Virgin carries a bowl of roses, and in front are three rose-filled *albarelli*. These rose-filled vases were adopted by later artists. As a result of the action of damp and the consequent deterioration of the altarpiece, it has proved necessary to remove the film of paint from all five panels, and this, studied from behind with the under-drawing uppermost, yields valuable information on the technical procedure by which Angelico's panels were built up (Pls. 32, 33). In each the forms are lightly sketched in *terra verde* on the priming, the linear features, hair, eyelids, nostrils, and lips being indicated with great refinement and subtlety. All of the under-drawing is by a single hand. While the under-drawing establishes the main areas of light and shadow, it has none of the heavy recession of the under-drawing in the triptych executed by Sassetta at about the same time for this church, and the volume of the completed figures is no more than hinted at. The process of completion involved some coarsening of the linear qualities of the cartoon. Comparison of the head of St John Baptist with the corresponding part of the cartoon beneath gives a fair impression of this impoverishment. In the case of the two outer figures, where this is particularly marked, studio intervention may be held responsible, but in the inner figures it is clear that Angelico himself deliberately sacrificed some of the beauty of the initial image to recession and solidity.

In composition the central panel of the Cortona altarpiece is closely related to that of a polyptych painted for the chapel of St Nicholas in the church of San Domenico at Perugia in 1437, now in the Galleria Nazionale at Perugia (Pls. 31, 34, 35). Dismantled before the middle of the nineteenth century, the panels of this altarpiece were later reintegrated in a modern frame. Originally the altarpiece was more compact, and the pilasters, now arranged in pairs of panels, must have been painted on two sides. Both the Virgin and Child and the fine figures of Saints Dominic and Nicholas of Bari on the left-hand side are less monumental than the comparable figures of the Linaiuoli tabernacle. The bowed head and open book of the St Nicholas seem to have influenced the St Augustine in the Carnesecchi tabernacle of Domenico Veneziano, who must have seen the painting in Perugia in 1438. The right-hand panels of the polyptych present a contrast to those on the left, and the figures of Saints John Baptist and Catherine of Alexandria are largely studio work. In the solidly constructed throne and in the table covered with a cloth which runs behind each pair of Saints, we may sense an effort to escape from the tyranny of the gold ground. Like the lateral Saints, the three predella panels (Figs. 6–8) reveal a weakening of the Masacciesque influences that went to the making of the Linaiuoli triptych; the figures are represented on a greatly reduced scale, and no longer dominate the scenes, and the settings have a lightness and lucidity that look forward to Angelico's greatest achievement in narrative painting, the predella of the San Marco altarpiece.

Concurrently with the Perugia polyptych, Angelico must have begun work on the last and most important of the paintings executed for Fiesole, the *Coronation of the Virgin* in the Louvre (Pls. 38, 44, 45). This painting is described by Vasari: 'But among all the works of Fra Giovanni, he surpassed himself and displayed the full extent of his powers and knowledge of art in a panel in the same church to the left of the entrance door, containing Christ crowning Our Lady in the middle of a choir of angels and a multitude of saints, so numerous, so well executed and so varied in action and gesture that it is an unspeakable delight to regard them, for it appears that the spirits of these blessed ones in heaven cannot be otherwise than these, or to put it better, they could not be if they were corporeal, for all the saints there are not only life-like and endowed with sweet and delicate expressions, but the entire colouring appears to be the work of a saint or angel like themselves. For this reason the friar with justice was always known as Fra Giovanni Angelico.' Contemporaries who compared the altarpiece in San Domenico with the large *Coronation of the Virgin* painted by Lorenzo Monaco for Santa Maria degli Angeli two decades earlier would have been struck by its severely rational design. In the earlier painting the attendant saints kneel, outside time and space, above a rainbow strewn with stars; in the later the logic of space composition is protracted into paradise. Compositionally the *Coronation* in the Louvre is one of the first paintings to make use of an expedient which was later to gain general currency, that of kneeling figures turned inwards in the front plane of the painting to mediate between the onlooker and the central group; and in the latter the inorganic grouping of Lorenzo Monaco is replaced by a scheme, perhaps deriving from a Giottesque prototype, in which the Virgin kneels in profile before Christ to receive her sacramental crown.

It is understandable enough that Angelico should have drawn on a Giottesque original in planning the central figures of this altarpiece, but neither the Virgin nor the Christ can be credited to Angelico in their present form, and the altarpiece was evidently left unfinished and completed by a second hand. One reason for this conclusion is that the types employed in the altarpiece fall into two separate groups, and that only the first of these can be reconciled with the style of Fra Angelico. A second and more cogent reason is that, whereas the throne makes use of the empirical methods of space representation usual in Angelico's work during the fourteen-thirties, the paved floor in the foreground is constructed scientifically on the principles of linear perspective, and is technically more advanced than paintings executed by Angelico at a considerably later time. The principles employed in the foreground of the altarpiece are also applied in the six narrative scenes of the predella, which depend from the corresponding scenes of the predella of the Cortona polyptych. But once again the figures are considerably modified, and when we juxtapose the individual panels of the two cycles, the identity of the second hand becomes self-evident, for the idiom of the little scenes is that of the most gifted of the younger painters active in Florence in the second quarter of the century, Domenico Veneziano. Since Domenico Veneziano did not arrive in Florence till 1439, the painting cannot have been completed before this year, and was in all probability abandoned by Angelico in 1438, when work was begun on the frescoes in the convent of San Marco. So far as can be judged, Angelico, before abandoning the painting, had completed the tabernacle and all of the standing figures to right and left, with the exception of one angel playing a mandolin beside the throne, and it is these parts of the painting alone that are relevant to a study of his style. In common with almost all the panel paintings which he executed after the early thirties, their colour has the high key and transparent tones of an illuminated manuscript. 'Another mode of attaining supernatural character,' writes Ruskin of this aspect of the artist's work, 'is by purity

6. THE BIRTH OF SAINT NICHOLAS, THE VOCATION OF SAINT NICHOLAS, AND SAINT NICHOLAS AND THE THREE MAIDENS. Pinacoteca Vaticana.

7. SAINT NICHOLAS ADDRESSING AN IMPERIAL EMISSARY, AND SAINT NICHOLAS SAVING A SHIP AT SEA. Pinacoteca Vaticana.

8. SAINT NICHOLAS SAVING THREE MEN CONDEMNED TO EXECUTION, AND THE DEATH OF SAINT NICHOLAS. Galleria Nazionale dell'Umbria, Perugia.

of colour almost shadowless, no more darkness being allowed than is absolutely necessary for the explanation of the forms and vividness of the effect, enhanced, as far as may be, by use of gilding, enamel and other jewellery.' A generation later the 'creamy and edible' palette of the *Coronation* found a commentator of a very different stamp in Proust.

The altarpieces painted during the fourteen-thirties pose a problem peculiar to Angelico. This arises from the studio practice of adapting motifs and figures from Angelico's designs for use, in a more archaic context, in paintings which have often been regarded as prototypes, and not derivatives, of the compositions from which they depend. Among these are a *Coronation of the Virgin* from Santa Maria Nuova, now in the Uffizi (Fig. x), where a number of heads from the Louvre altarpiece are introduced into a loose, miniature-like design, and a small *Coronation of the Virgin* in the Museo di San Marco (Fig. xxxix), one of four reliquary panels from Santa Maria Novella, of which two, the *Madonna della Stella* (Fig. xxxvii) and the *Annunciation and Adoration of the Magi* (Fig. xxxviii), are also at San Marco, and one, the *Burial and Assumption of the Virgin* (Fig. xl), is at Boston. All of these panels are by a single hand. The same artist was responsible for executing, about 1435–40, the *Last Judgment* seen by Vasari at Santa Maria degli Angeli and now in the Museo di San Marco (Fig. xxxii). In this case Angelico's original is lost, and we are left to reconstruct from what can be no more than a free variant a design which was as influential in the history of *Last Judgment* iconography as were the Cortona and Fiesole altarpieces in the history of their themes. Later works by the same painter are the variants of the Cortona *Annunciation* at Montecarlo (about 1445) and at Madrid (about 1455). There are good grounds for supposing that the author of these paintings was the miniaturist Zanobi Strozzi, who is mentioned by Vasari as a disciple of Angelico and is said to have 'made paintings for the whole of Florence for the houses of the citizens'. Zanobi Strozzi was born in 1412 and died in 1468, and his style is known to us from a number of manuscripts illuminated for San Marco and San Domenico at Fiesole. Two miniaturists with whom he collaborated, Battista di Biagio Sanguigni and Filippo di Matteo Torelli, may also have executed panel paintings in the orbit of Angelico. Another pupil of Angelico, as yet unidentified, makes his first appearance in the predella of the Cortona polyptych. A less appealing artist than Zanobi Strozzi, this painter is more at ease on a large than a small scale, and by 1438 had absorbed sufficient of the master's style to become Angelico's principal assistant in the frescoes at San Marco.

★   ★   ★

The recall of Cosimo de' Medici to Florence in 1434 opened a new chapter in the history of the Dominican Observance at Fiesole. As early as 1420 Cosimo had exercised his patronage in favour of the reformed Franciscan convent of Bosco ai Frati, and two years after his return he secured the assent of the Pope, Eugenius IV, then resident in Florence, to the requisitioning and handing over to the Observant Dominican community of the Silvestrine convent of San Marco. Important for the community, this formal alliance with the Medici was important also for Angelico. Of the three altarpieces which follow the Perugia polyptych, two were certainly, and one was probably, commissioned by Cosimo de' Medici. Unlike the Cortona and Perugia polyptychs, uneasy in their compromise between an old art and a new, these three altarpieces are painted on single panels, and form a logical progression, first in respect of composition, in that each scene is thrust further back into the picture space, and secondly in interpretation, in that the emotional barrier between the figures is gradually reduced. In these paintings we can follow the stages by which the old-fashioned polyptych was transformed into the *sacra conversazione* of the later fifteenth century. The first of the three altarpieces, now in the Museo di San Marco, comes from the Dominican convent of San Vincenzo d'Annalena, and seems to have been painted about 1437. The second was executed for the high altar of San Marco, on the commission of Cosimo de' Medici, between 1438 and 1440, and the third was painted for the Franciscan church of San Buonaventura at Bosco ai Frati, near the Medici villa of Cafaggiolo, before 1445.

In the Annalena altarpiece (Pls. 36, 37) the niche in which the Virgin sits recalls that of the Perugia polyptych. But the platform of the throne is extended to right and left across the whole width of the panel, and a new architectural feature is introduced in the form of an arcaded wall from which the throne projects. The extended platform enables the six saints, who are arranged in a receding line three on each side, to be brought into direct relationship with the central group. The challenge presented by the architectural setting, however, (and for an artist accustomed to the relative space of the gold ground this was a challenge indeed) is evaded by the use of a brocaded curtain with its top line slightly above the heads of the six saints. Six scenes from the legend of Saints Cosmas and Damian in the Museo di San Marco (Fig. IX) and a seventh panel in the Spencer-Churchill collection, all executed by Zanobi Strozzi, probably formed the predella of this altarpiece.

Vasari's life of Fra Angelico includes a brief account of the San Marco altarpiece: 'But especially beautiful and marvellous is the picture on the high altar of the church. The Madonna inspires devotion in the beholder by her simplicity, and the saints who stand around her do likewise. The predella, in which there are stories from the martyrdom of Saints Cosmas and Damian and their companions, is so well done that it is impossible to imagine one can ever see a thing made with more diligence, nor figures more delicate or better understood than these.' The main panel (Pls. 39–43) is so greatly abraded that it is difficult to-day to visualize the effect it must originally have made, and we must turn to the nine predella panels, most of which are well preserved, for an impression of the jewel-like brilliance of the altarpiece (Pls. 46–55; Figs. 9, 10). The throne,

9. THE HEALING OF PALLADIA BY SAINTS COSMAS AND DAMIAN, AND SAINT DAMIAN RECEIVING A GIFT FROM PALLADIA. National Gallery of Art, Washington (Kress Collection).

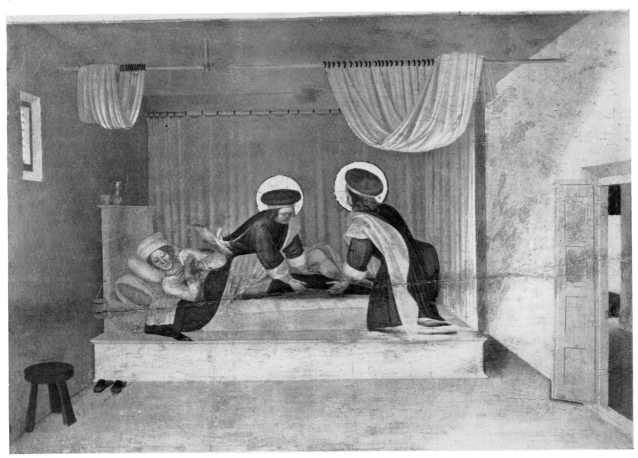

10. THE DREAM OF THE DEACON JUSTINIAN. Museo di San Marco, Florence.

which includes a new feature in the Corinthian pilasters supporting the pediment, runs to the full height of the panel, and the Virgin and Child, like the six saints of the Annalena altarpiece, are represented not against the architecture, but before a gold-brocaded curtain stretched across the niche. To right and left is a low wall hung with a curtain, which serves as background for the saints on either side. These are disposed in two receding lines. In the foreground are the kneeling figures of Saints Cosmas and Damian, one turned to the spectator and gesticulating towards the central group, the other gazing at the Child. A number of devices is used to increase the space illusion. The first of these is the Anatolian carpet in the foreground with its sharply receding orthogonals and carefully demarcated planes. This feature recurs in the San Giusto alle Mura altarpiece of Ghirlandaio and many other paintings. The second is the line of cypresses and palm trees seen on each side beyond the wall. This part of the painting was imitated by Baldovinetti in the Cafaggiolo altarpiece in the Uffizi. A third device is the looped gold curtains which enclose the foreground like a proscenium. These served as models for paintings by Raffaellino del Garbo, Verrocchio, and other artists.

A letter written to Piero de' Medici by the young Domenico Veneziano in April 1438 testifies to the reputation that Angelico enjoyed in Florence at this time. It reads: 'I have heard just now that Cosimo is determined to have executed, that is painted, an altarpiece, and requires magnificent work. This news pleases me much, and would please me still more if it were possible for you to ensure through your magnanimity that I painted it. If this comes about, I hope in God to show you marvellous things, even considering that there are good masters, like Fra Filippo and Fra Giovanni, who have much work to do.' In the light of the last sentence it is interesting to compare the San Marco altarpiece with a painting commissioned from Filippo Lippi in 1437, the Barbadori altarpiece from Santo Spirito, now in the Louvre. The Barbadori altarpiece shows a facility in the handling of space and the drawing of architecture which is nowhere to be found in the painting at San Marco. But Lippi's baroque style, with its Donatellesque volume, its emphasis on movement and its play of line, is a secular manifestation, whereas that of Angelico, more concentrated and composed, is directed solely to devotional ends. It must have been precisely this intellectual repose, the immutable gestures and careful space relationships, that won for the San Marco altarpiece its place as the archetype of so many Florentine religious paintings.

The eight scenes from the legend of Saints Cosmas and Damian in the predella are the most distinguished and most graphic of Angelico's narrative paintings. Like the main panel of the altarpiece, the predella employs a new compositional device, in the form of a flat wall surface parallel with the front plane of the painting against which the principal figures are set. This device is used in the two panels from the predella in the Museo di San Marco (*A Miracle of Saints Cosmas and Damian* and *The Burial of Saints Cosmas and Damian*), a panel in Washington (*The Healing of Palladia by Saints Cosmas and Damian*), two panels in Munich (*Saints Cosmas and Damian before Lycias*, and *Lycias possessed by Devils and Saints Cosmas and Damian thrown into the Sea*), and one at Dublin (*The attempted Martyrdom of Saints Cosmas and Damian by Fire*). Over and above its value as a method of securing emphasis, this results in compositions which are more concentrated than those of the predella at Perugia. The figure drawing is characterized by the same interest in movement and the same recourse to visual distortions as in the Perugia predella, from which two scenes, the left half of that in Washington and the *Decapitation of Saints Cosmas and Damian* in the Louvre depend. Like the Perugia panels, the predella of the San Marco altarpiece has sometimes been denied to Fra Angelico, but given the destination of the altarpiece, there is a high degree of probability that Angelico was himself responsible for the bulk of these small panels, and it is likely that the ease in the rendering of movement and the confident and accomplished compositions of the scenes represent a new phase in the master's evolution, and not the contribution of some younger artist. To-day, as we review the detail in the nine surviving panels – the bowls of flowers above the wall in the Munich *Saints Cosmas and Damian before Lycias*, the distant hills in the *Crucifixion of Saints Cosmas and Damian*, the rippling sea of the *Lycias possessed by Devils*, the line of poplars in the Louvre panel outlined against an evening sky, the wrinkled winding street of the *Entombment* and the Piero-like buildings of the concluding scene – it is difficult to contest the view that, when assembled, this was the most beautiful predella in the whole of quattrocento painting.

The Bosco ai Frati altarpiece (Pl. 69) contains a synthesis of elements from the Annalena and San Marco paintings. The design, with its wide central niche, is ampler than that of the Annalena altarpiece, and the four Saints, on the left Saints Francis and Anthony of Padua and on the right Saints Cosmas and Peter Martyr, represented for the first time against the architectural background without an intervening curtain of brocade, are shown in the same gentle colloquy as the saints in the San Marco altarpiece. In its original position over the high altar of the church, this painting conformed closely to the scheme completed there by Michelozzo in 1438, and its spacious composition hints for the first time at a relationship pregnant with possibilities. Writers on Angelico have associated with this altarpiece a much-restored predella, now distributed between Berlin, the Vatican and Altenburg (Figs. XII–XVI), containing at the outer ends the two scenes of *The Meeting of Saints Francis and Dominic* and *The Stigmatization of Saint Francis*, and between them three panels with scenes from the life of St Francis. A long central panel with *The Death of Saint Francis* is based on the fresco by Giotto in Santa Croce.

In a number of respects the San Marco predella adumbrates the style of two altarpieces which seem to have been executed after 1440. One of these is a *Deposition*, now in the Museo di San Marco (Pls. 57–66), which was seen by Vasari in the sacristy of Santa Trinità; the other is a *Lamentation over the Dead Christ*, also in the Museo di San Marco, which was painted for the

Compagnia del Tempio (Pls. 67, 68; Fig. 11). The *Deposition* is painted on a single panel surmounted by three finials by Lorenzo Monaco. In shape it recalls another altarpiece painted for Santa Trinità, Gentile da Fabriano's *Adoration of the Magi*, and this, in conjunction with Lorenzo Monaco's close association with the church, suggests that Angelico's task was to complete an altarpiece commissioned from the older artist. Though the composition is deployed across the entire panel, the figures fall into three separate groups. In the centre the body of Christ is let down from the cross. Two ladders form a rectangle which serves to isolate the central group. Like the figure of Lycias in two of the panels of the San Marco predella at Munich, the Christ is shown with arms outstretched, filling the whole of the centre of the scene. One of the two figures letting down the body from the cross, the Nicodemus, is said by Vasari to represent the architect Michelozzo; but if Michelozzo is represented in the group, this is more probably in the head of a man wearing a black *cappuccio* below the Christ's right arm. Beneath, the body is received by an older male figure and by St John. The group is completed by the Magdalen, kissing the feet of Christ, and by a kneeling Beato, perhaps San Giovanni Gualberto, the founder of the Vallombrosan Order to which the church belonged. Like the kneeling saints of the San Marco altarpiece, this figure, with eyes fixed on the central group and hand extended towards the onlooker, marks the transition from the real world of the spectator to the false world of the picture space. In the halo of Christ appear the words CORONA GLORIE, and below is a quotation from the eighty-seventh Psalm: ESTIMATVS SVM CVM DESCENDENTIBVS IN LACVM. To the left are the holy women, in their centre the Virgin kneeling behind the winding sheet, and on the right is a group of male figures, one of them exhibiting the nails and crown of thorns. In the halo of the Virgin are the words: VIRGO MARIA N(ON) E(ST) T(IBI) SIMILIS, and beneath is the inscription: PLANGENT EVM QVASI VNIGENITVM QVIA INOCENS, while under the right side of the painting appears the verse: ECCE QVOMODO MORITVR IVSTVS ET NEMO PERCIPIT CORDE. The deliberate avoidance of the realistic detail proper to a simple narrative of the *Deposition*, the tender gestures with which the figures in the centre perform their ritual, and the restraint of the spectators, consumed by inner sorrow which finds expression in sympathetic lassitude rather than in rhetoric, are explained by the inscriptions, which lend the painting the character of a homily rather than of a narrative. The crown of glory won by the sacrifice of Christ, the sorrow of the Virgin with which no human sorrow can compare, the lament of the women for the innocent victim on the Cross as for their only sons, and the body of the Saviour, instinct with the promise of the Resurrection, all these are phases in a meditation on the sufferings of Christ.

The much repainted *Lamentation* from the Dominican church of Croce al Tempio (Fig. 11) is inseparable from the *Deposition*. Here the historical figures of the Virgin, supporting the head of Christ, St John, raising His left hand, the Magdalen, at His feet, and Joseph of Arimathaea and Nicodemus, behind His head, are accompanied by the Beata Villana (a Florentine saint over whose relics the Compagnia del Tempio held certain rights) and Saints Dominic and Catherine of Alexandria. The life of the Beata Villana extracted by Razzi from a volume of biographies of the Saints and Beati of the Dominican Order tells us how ardently the Beata aspired to share the sufferings of her celestial spouse, and how 'in her visions she had always before her mind the image of her Jesus Christ, beaten and crucified, whose torments she wished to emulate'. In these circumstances it is likely that the painting represents not (as is generally assumed) the lamentation over the dead Christ with a number of ancillary figures, but a meditation, in which the Beata, accompanied by St Catherine, who had appeared to her in visions, and by the founder of her Order, St. Dominic, takes part in spirit in the tragic scene. This is confirmed by the single inscription on the panel, an exclamation issuing from the Beata's mouth which reads: CRISTO IESV LAMOR MIO CRVCIFISSO. Those parts of the painting which are by Fra Angelico are closely similar to the corresponding parts of the *Deposition*, but the handling of much of the panel is of lower quality and is evidently by the same studio assistant who was responsible for the heads

11. THE LAMENTATION OVER THE DEAD CHRIST.
Museo di San Marco, Florence.

of the three women in the larger altarpiece. Though the mystical content of the two pictures is essentially the same, the Croce al Tempio altarpiece makes the effect of an extemporized design, and is of interest principally as a touchstone by which the artistic quality of the *Deposition* can be assessed.

Some of the most enchanting features of the predella panels from San Marco are the landscape backgrounds, which for the first time play a major part in the designs. These landscape backgrounds recur on a larger scale in the *Lamentation* and *Deposition* in the Museo di San Marco. From these paintings Fra Angelico emerges as one of the great landscape painters of the fifteenth century. In so far as it is consciously designed to impose a unity of mood throughout the panel, Angelico's is an ideal landscape, and his paintings offer us not a portrayal of some specific scene, but a generalized image of the Tuscan countryside. Yet this accretion of detail, these grey-brown hills receding into space, these horizontal lines of cloud, these Corot-like wall surfaces warmed by the setting sun, betray an innate interest in visual appearances. Though later artists achieved more faithful and more realistic transcriptions of the Tuscan landscape, none conveys better than Angelico the sense of its idyllic quietude.

Concurrently with these altarpieces Angelico must have begun work on the frescoes in the convent of San Marco. The sequence of the buildings at San Marco can be established with a fair measure of certainty from the *Cronaca di San Marco* compiled by Giuliano Lappaccini, a companion of Angelico who received the habit of the order at Fiesole in 1436 and in 1444 became Prior of San Marco. When the Dominicans took over the premises in 1436, the convent buildings were in ruins, and only the church was structurally sound. Since the Dominican title to the convent was contested by the Silvestrine community, rebuilding did not start till 1437, and for two years the friars were housed in damp cells and wooden huts. When the Council of Basle at length gave its decision in favour of the Dominican claim to the convent, the task of reconstruction was

begun, and from this time on work was pressed forward at the commission of the Medici by the
architect and sculptor Michelozzo. In 1439 the *cappella maggiore* of the church was finished, and
by 1442 the church was ready to be dedicated. The rebuilding of the convent premises was pro-
ceeded with at the same time. In 1437 twenty cells were rebuilt or repaired, and by 1443 all the
cells on the upper floor, to a total of forty-four, were fit for habitation. Structural work in one
part of the building or another continued till 1452. We do not know in what year the frescoes in
the convent were begun, but this can hardly have been before 1438. Close contact must have been
maintained between Angelico and Michelozzo during the years in which the convent was being
built. The fruits of this are to be found first in the new understanding of architectural forms which
is evident in the predella of the San Marco altarpiece and which distinguishes the setting of the
Bosco ai Frati altarpiece from that of earlier paintings, and secondly in the San Marco frescoes,
where the settings depend for their effect upon the same unerring use of interval as do the cloister
and library of Michelozzo.

Describing the most notable features of the convent, Lappaccini mentions the Library (con-
spicuous alike for its great length and for its thirty-two benches of cypress wood), the residential
buildings (so harmonious yet so convenient), and the garden, and goes on: 'A third feature is the
paintings. For the altarpiece of the high altar and the figures in the Sala del Capitolo and the first
cloister and all the upper cells and the Crucifixion in the refectory are all painted by the brother
of the Dominican Order from the convent at Fiesole, who had the highest mastery in the art of
painting in Italy. He was called Brother Johannes Petri de Mugello, and was a man of the utmost
modesty and of religious life.' The frescoes on the ground floor of the convent comprise a *Christ
on the Cross adored by Saint Dominic* and five lunettes in the cloister, and a large *Crucifixion with
attendant Saints* in the Sala del Capitolo. A fresco of the *Crucifixion* in the refectory was destroyed
in 1554. On the first floor are three frescoes in the corridor (a *Christ on the Cross adored by Saint
Dominic*, an *Annunciation* and a *Virgin and Child with Saints*) and forty-three frescoes in the forty-
five cells opening off it. All the frescoes on the ground floor are wholly or partly by Angelico. On
the extent of his responsibility for the remaining frescoes a wide variety of view has been expressed,
and at one time or another he has been credited with as many as forty-one and as few as six of
the narrative scenes. The *Cronaca di San Marco* proves beyond all reasonable doubt that as early
as 1457 (the terminal date for the completion of the chronicle) Angelico was credited with the
entire fresco decoration of the convent as it then stood. But this view is sanctioned neither by
examination of the frescoes nor by common sense, for the execution of so many frescoes in
so short a time was manifestly beyond the capacity of a single artist, and the frescoes themselves reveal the presence of at least three main hands. That the class of fresco painted in
the cells was ideated by Angelico and that Angelico himself supervised the decoration of the
convent is not open to doubt, but the frescoes for which the master was directly responsible are
vastly outnumbered by the scenes in which assistants were charged with executing his cartoons,
or which were conceived by studio hands within the framework of his style.

The *Scenes from the Life of Christ* which decorate the cells follow no natural sequence. Frescoes
whose subjects are inter-related are sometimes separated by the whole length of the corridor, and
the choice of scenes appears to have been arbitrary. The frescoes in the eleven cells on the east
side of the corridor represent the *Noli Me tangere*, the *Entombment*, the *Annunciation*, *Christ on the
Cross with four Saints*, the *Nativity*, the *Transfiguration*, the *Mocking of Christ*, the *Resurrection*, the
Coronation of the Virgin, the *Presentation in the Temple*, and the *Virgin and Child with two Saints*.
With the exception of a fresco of the *Adoration of the Magi* in Cell 39 on the north-west corner of
the building, these include the only frescoes in the cells for which a direct attribution to Angelico
is warranted. Even these scenes vary appreciably in quality, but applying criteria based on his other
works and on the frescoes below, we may credit Angelico with the design and execution of
the *Noli Me tangere* in Cell 1, the *Annunciation* in Cell 3, the *Transfiguration* in Cell 6, the *Mocking*

of Christ in Cell 7, the *Coronation of the Virgin* in Cell 9, and the *Presentation in the Temple* in Cell 10. The frescoes in Cells 2, 4, 5, 8 and 11 are by a single hand, the Master of Cell 2. All of these five frescoes were executed under the general direction of Angelico, and incorporate motifs by the master, who was not, however, responsible for the cartoons. An indication of the close association that must have existed between Angelico and his disciple is afforded by the presence in the *Annunciation* in Cell 3 of a figure of St Peter Martyr painted by the Master of Cell 2, and in the *Maries at the Sepulchre* in Cell 8 of an angel's head painted by Angelico. The Master of Cell 2 seems to have been a member of the master's studio from the mid-thirties on, and was responsible for the predella of the polyptych at Cortona and for parts of the Croce al Tempio *Lamentation* and of the *Deposition* from Santa Trinità.

The frescoes in the cells on the inner side of the corridor overlooking the cloister are greatly inferior to the frescoes in the outer cells. Cells 15 to 22 contain figures of *Christ on the Cross adored by Saint Dominic*, which depend from the frescoes of this subject by Angelico in the cloister beneath and by a studio assistant in the corridor; these are largely the work of a single artist, and maintain a level of undistinguished competence. They are followed, in Cells 24, 25, 26, 27 and 28, by five scenes (the *Baptism of Christ, Christ on the Cross*, the *Man of Sorrows*, the *Flagellation* and *Christ carrying the Cross*), which are almost certainly by the Master of Cell 2, but are less closely indebted to Angelico than the frescoes opposite, and were perhaps executed after 1447 when Angelico left Florence. Turning the corner, along the north side of the cloister we come to six scenes by a single hand (*Christ in Limbo*, the *Sermon on the Mount*, the *Arrest of Christ*, the *Temptation of Christ*, the *Agony in the Garden* and the *Institution of the Eucharist*), where the loose grouping and curvilinear compositions are totally at variance with the frescoes in the earlier cells. These frescoes may be somewhat later in date than the other frescoes in the cells, and have no direct relevance to the style of Angelico. Passing to Cells 36, 37 and 42, we find a fresco of *Christ nailed to the Cross* and two frescoes of the *Crucifixion*, in which the spirit, if not the handling, once more conforms to Angelico's intentions. The author of these scenes followed Angelico to Rome in 1447 and was employed in the upper cycle of frescoes in the Vatican. The much restored *Adoration of the Magi* in Cell 39 (which is considerably larger than the other cells, and was occupied by Cosimo de' Medici, Pope Eugenius IV and other distinguished visitors to the convent) was designed, and in all probability partly executed, by Angelico.

There is no evidence for the order in which the frescoes were produced. It is likely that those publicly accessible were completed before those designed for private meditation in the cells. The *Adoration of the Magi* probably precedes the frescoes in the other cells, since it was carried out in part by the same hand which was responsible for the figures in the border of the *Crucifixion* in the Sala del Capitolo, and like the *Crucifixion* may have been painted on the commission of Cosimo de' Medici. It is a reasonable hypothesis that the frescoes in Cells 1–11 and 36, 37, 39 and 42 were completed by the time Angelico left Florence for Rome in 1446–7, and that the remaining frescoes were undertaken, in his absence, in part by former members of his studio, in part by independent artists. Two of the frescoes in the corridor, the *Annunciation* and the *Virgin and Child with Saints*, are certainly later in date than the other scenes, and were probably designed and executed by Angelico after his return from Rome in 1449.

The largest of the frescoes in the cloister, that opposite the entrance, shows *Christ on the Cross adored by Saint Dominic* (Pls. 71, 72). Developed from the fresco in the Louvre, it establishes the central theme of the frescoes on the upper as well as on the lower floor, the mystical participation of members of the Dominican Order, personified by the figure of their founder, in the life and sufferings of Christ. The shape of the fresco field was changed in the seventeenth century, when an irregular marble surround was added to it. By comparison with the fresco from Fiesole, the body of Christ is modelled with a new richness, and the head, with its arched eyebrows and closed eyes, has the same grave simplicity as the head of Christ in the *Deposition* altarpiece. The five lunettes in the cloister are in poor condition. Four of them, the *Saint Peter Martyr* enjoining silence above the entrance to the sacristy (Pl. 76), the much abraded *Saint Dominic* holding out his rule, the *Saint Thomas Aquinas* with the *Summa* open on his breast (Pl. 75), and the *Christ as Man of Sorrows* (Pl. 73), are distinguished principally for their sense of volume and for the masterly placing of the figures on their grounds, while the fifth, above the doorway of the hospice, shows *Christ as Pilgrim received by two Dominicans* (Pl. 74), and affords a foretaste of the narrative treatment of the frescoes on the upper floor.

A work of greater intrinsic importance is the *Crucifixion* in the Sala del Capitolo (Pls. 78–82; Fig. 12). This large semi-circular fresco fills the entire north wall of the room. Its programme emerges from the pages of Vasari, who relates how Angelico was instructed by Cosimo de' Medici 'to paint the Passion of Christ on a wall of the chapter-house. On one side are all the saints who have founded or been heads of religious orders, sorrowful and weeping at the foot of the Cross, the other side being occupied by St Mark the Evangelist, the Mother of God, who has fainted on seeing the Saviour of the world crucified, the Maries who are supporting her, and Saints Cosmas and Damian, the former said to be a portrait of his friend Nanni d'Antonio di Banco, the sculptor. Beneath this work, in a frieze above the dado, he made a tree, at the foot of which is St Dominic; and in some medallions, which are about the branches, are all the popes, cardinals, bishops, saints and masters of theology who had been members of the Order of the Friars Preachers up to that time. In this work he introduced many portraits, the friars helping him by sending for them to different places.' Like the Croce al Tempio *Lamentation*, the fresco at San Marco is a mystical representation of the Crucifixion and not a narrative scene. The figures of the crucified Christ, the women beneath the cross, and the attendant saints (on the left Saints Cosmas and Damian, Lawrence, Mark and John the Baptist, on the right Saints Dominic, once more kneeling beneath the Cross, Ambrose, Jerome, Augustine, Francis, Benedict, Bernard, Giovanni Gualberto, Peter Martyr and Thomas Aquinas) are ranged along the front plane of the painting, and the single intimation of space is in the crosses of the two thieves which recede diagonally into the dark ground. The vertical shaft of the Cross divides the fresco into two equal halves, and fills the whole height of the lunette. The theme of the painting is elaborated in inscriptions on the scrolls held by the prophets in the decorative border surrounding the scene. Among these are the VERE LANGORES NOSTROS IPSE TVLIT ET DOLORES NOSTROS of Isaiah, the O VOS OMNES QVI TRANSITE PER VIAM ATTENDITE ET VIDETE SI EST DOLOR SICVT DOLOR MEVS of Jeremiah, and the QVIS DET DE CARNIBVS EIVS VT SATVREMVR of Job. An impressive exposition of an intellectual concept, the *Crucifixion* is not one of Angelico's most successful paintings, and owing in part to its condition (the original blue ground has been removed, leaving the much repainted figures like cut-out silhouettes on the red underpainting) and in part to the weight of its didactic scheme, it remains a manifesto which falls short of a great work of art.

Those who know the frescoes in the cells upstairs only from photographs miss their essential character. In relation to the rooms in which they find themselves, most of the scenes (and all of those associable with Angelico) are relatively large in scale. In each case the scene is represented on the window wall opposite the door, and the wall thus contains two apertures, one opening on the physical and the other on the spiritual world. Dominating their austere surroundings, they were designed as aids to meditation, and not as decoration, and were intended to secure for the mysteries they described a place in the forefront of the friar's mind by keeping them constantly before his eyes. In this respect they form a spiritual exercise. The cursory examination of the frescoes which we make as we walk from cell to cell to-day is the exact opposite of the use for which they were designed. At Fiesole the frescoed decoration of the convent seems to have been confined to public rooms, and there is no evidence to whom we owe the decision to extend this decoration to the cells occupied by individual friars. Perhaps the decision was taken by Fra Cipriano, the first prior of San Marco, perhaps by Sant'Antonino, who recommends the

12. SAINT JOHN THE BAPTIST AND THE HOLY WOMEN. (Detail of Plate 78 before restoration.)
San Marco, Florence.

contemplation of devotional pictures as one of the reasons why the faithful should pay frequent visits to a church. But it is indicative of Angelico's contribution to this conception that the simplest and sparsest of the frescoes in the cells are those for which he was responsible, while those in which he had no hand revert, by some process of natural attraction, to the norm of fresco painting.

One of the finest of the autograph frescoes on the upper floor is the *Annunciation* in the third cell (Pls. 83, 86). Here almost all of the characteristic features of the *Annunciation* at Cortona and of the paintings based on it are abandoned in favour of a composition of the utmost severity. Instead of the Brunelleschan loggia of the earlier painting, with its garden and doorway leading into another room, it depicts a cell-like chamber closed by a blind wall, which has the double function of providing a background for the figures and of discouraging the mind from straying from the confines of the scene. It is characteristic of a tendency to eliminate extraneous detail that even the capitals of the two columns are covered by the angel's wings. Alberti in his theory of architecture distinguishes between Beauty and Ornament, the one deriving from a system of harmonious proportion, the other consisting of the columns and other ancillary decorative features of the building. Angelico's consistent avoidance in the frescoes in the cells of architectural features which Alberti would have considered ornamental, and his rigid adherence to a system of visual harmony, suggests that at San Marco he may have had some such distinction in mind. The Michelozzan vaulting above, realized with the finality of an abstract pattern, is not the least beautiful aspect of the fresco. In the figures the intimation of movement which contributes so much to the appeal of the earlier altarpiece is put aside, and the Virgin and angel are treated like a sculptured group, restrained and motionless.

The *Noli Me tangere* in the first cell (Pls. 84, 85) follows the same compositional procedure as the *Annunciation*. Once again the visual interest of the scheme depends on the relation between two figures in repose, and once again a flat surface, in this case a wooden paling, is used to isolate the head of the main figure. This scene is the only one of Angelico's cell frescoes into which there obtrudes the interest in nature, the plethora of minutely observed and carefully rendered flowers, grasses and trees, that we find in the *Deposition* altarpiece and other panel paintings. In the *Nativity* in the fifth cell (Fig. xx), where the figures are backed by the firm rectangle of the stable and the heads of the Virgin and St Joseph are set against a wicker door, the composition once more recalls Angelico. The sixth cell brings us to what is in some respects the greatest of the frescoes, the *Transfiguration* (Pls. 93–96), where the majestic figure of Christ, with arms out-stretched in a pose prefiguring the Crucifixion, is outlined against a wheel of light. Beneath this splendid frontal figure, so clearly reminiscent of the Christ from Michelozzo's Aragazzi monu-ment, there crouch the three apostles in poses instinct with astonishment and awe. The heads of Moses and Elias beneath the arms of Christ illustrate very clearly the strength of modelling of which Angelico was capable throughout these frescoes. The *Mocking of Christ* (Pls. 87, 88) shows the central figure seated, again in full face, against a rectangle of curtain, on which are depicted the symbols of His suffering. The use of this emblematic iconography, for which precedents occur in the trecento, may have been dictated by the wish to avoid violent action and strong narrative interest in these frescoes. Few forms in the frescoes are realized with greater sureness and accomplishment than the white robe of Christ. Seated on a low step in the foreground are the contemplative figures of the Virgin and St Dominic, the former wholly, the latter in part by the studio assistant responsible for the second, fourth and fifth scenes. This hand appears once more in the *Maries at the Sepulchre* in the eighth cell (Fig. xxi), where the figure of the Virgin peering down into the tomb seems to have been designed, and the head of the angel was almost certainly executed, by Angelico. In the left-hand corner of the fresco a praying figure of St Dominic fulfils the same function as the St Peter Martyr in the *Annunciation*. The *Coronation of the Virgin* in the ninth cell (Pls. 91, 92) is strikingly at variance with Angelico's earlier paintings of this theme, for the act of coronation is performed not, as in the painting in the Louvre and the panels which depend from it, before a host of onlookers, but in isolation, with six kneeling saints who proclaim, but do not assist in, the main scene. With the *Transfiguration*, this noble design forms one of the peaks of Angelico's art. Apart from these frescoes stands the much-restored lunette of the *Adoration of the Magi* in Cell 39 (Pl. 77). In design and handling this fresco is more closely related to the *Crucifixion* in the Sala del Capitolo than to the frescoes in the cells, for not only is the deployment of the figures in a frieze along the front plane of the painting essentially the same, but certain of the figures, particularly those on the right, seem to have been executed by the same assistant who was responsible for parts of the larger scene. This assistant has sometimes been identified with the young Benozzo Gozzoli. A number of the poses used in the *Adoration* are anticipated in the predella of the San Marco altarpiece, and both the elaborate, studied composition and the light, decorative palette of the fresco are more secular in spirit than the small scenes in the cells.

★ ★ ★

After four years or more of work on the frescoes in the convent and on other commissions, Angelico's quiet and productive life within the confines of San Marco was interrupted by a summons to the papal court. According to Vasari, this summons came from Pope Nicholas V, but since the first reference to Angelico's presence in Rome dates from as little as six days after Nicholas V's election on 6 March 1447, it is almost certain that the invitation was issued by his predecessor, Pope Eugenius IV. There are other reasons for believing that this must have been so. A sponsor of the Observant movement, Eugenius IV had lived for upwards of ten years in Florence, and in 1443 was himself present at the consecration of San Marco, when 'for the consolation of the friars in the convent he remained there the whole day, and spent the night in sleep in the first cell looking over the second cloister, which is now called the cell of Cosimo'. Whether or not the *Adoration of the Magi* in this cell was completed by the time of the Pope's visit, Eugenius must have been familiar both with the artist and with his many works in Florence. There is a tradition that in 1445 the Pope offered the vacant Archbishopric of Florence to Fra Angelico, and that the latter, refusing the proposed preferment, recommended the appointment of the Prior of San Marco, Sant'Antonino. If this tradition were correct, it would imply that Angelico was employed in Rome before March 1445, when Sant'Antonino's translation took effect. But if, as is more likely, it is a fiction invented by some pious hagiographer, we may presume that Angelico reached Rome late in 1446 or early in the following year.

The Rome of 1446 was no longer the desolate city to which Pope Martin V had returned a quarter of a century before. The pagan Pantheon had been restored, and a long line of artists from Central and North Italy (Masaccio and Masolino in San Clemente and Santa Maria Maggiore, Gentile da Fabriano and Pisanello in the Lateran basilica, Donatello and Filarete in St Peter's) had set their seal upon its monuments. The Vatican had not yet taken its place as the main scene of activity for artists in the papal city, and the work undertaken in the palace by Angelico forms the opening phase in a campaign of decoration and improvement which was to be pursued uninterruptedly until the Sack of Rome. The documents referring to Angelico's work in the Vatican are more explicit than some writers on the artist have supposed. Between 9 May and 1 June 1447 three documents refer to payments for work 'nela chapella di so Pietro'. In May an arrangement was made, no doubt with the sanction of Nicholas V, whereby Angelico spent the summer months at Orvieto, decorating the Cappella di San Brizio in the Cathedral. During June, July, August and the first half of September the master and his assistants were employed upon this work. The document from which we learn the terms of this commission is dated 11 May 1447, and mentions in parenthesis that at this time Angelico was engaged in painting the 'cappellam Smi. D.N. in palatio apostolico sancti Petri de Urbe', or the Pope's private chapel in the Vatican. In view of the coincidence of date, we are bound to assume that this is identical with the commission noted in the Roman documents, and that the term 'chapel of St Peter' is an abbreviation of the full title given in the Orvieto contract, the 'chapel of His Holiness Our Lord the Pope in the apostolic palace of St Peter's'. There can thus be no reasonable doubt that the only surviving work painted by Angelico in Rome, the frescoed decoration of the Chapel of Nicholas V in the Vatican, was under way in the spring of 1447. The decoration of the chapel was probably completed by the end of 1448, for by 1 January 1449 Angelico was engaged on another apartment in the Vatican, the 'studio di N.S.' or study of Nicholas V. This room, which had the double function of workroom and library, seems to have been adjacent to the Chapel. Work in the study must have been less extensive than that in the Chapel, for it appears to have been finished by June 1449, when Gozzoli, Angelico's principal assistant, returned to Orvieto. In the second half of 1449 Angelico was elected Prior of San Domenico and left Rome for Fiesole.

Throughout his years in Rome Angelico must have been on terms of intimacy with the Pope in whose apartments he was employed. As Tommaso Parentucelli, Nicholas V had won fame as a scholar and bibliophile, and during his pontificate the papal court at Rome became a centre of humanistic studies. 'All the scholars of the world,' writes Vespasiano da Bisticci, 'came to Rome in the time of Pope Nicholas, some of them on their own initiative, others at his invitation since he wished to see them at his court.' 'Under what pontiff,' asks Birago in his *Strategicon adversus Turcos*, 'was this throne more splendid or magnificent?' The humanistic interests of Nicholas V found expression in his patronage of architecture and in his conservation of the monuments of Rome, but seem not to have influenced his taste in painting; in addition to Angelico, two Umbrian painters, Bartolommeo di Tommaso da Foligno and Benedetto Bonfigli, were employed at the papal court. For Angelico, however, trained in the sequestered precincts of San Domenico and San Marco under the gaunt shadow of Dominici, the court of Nicholas V, with its wide intellectual horizons, represented a new world, the impact of which can be traced in the frescoes in the papal chapel.

Filling three sides of a small room, these consist of three lunettes, containing six scenes from the life of St Stephen, and three rectangular frescoes beneath, containing five scenes from the life of St Lawrence. Flanking the frescoes on the lateral walls are eight full-length figures of the Fathers of the Church, and on the roof (Fig. 13) are the four Evangelists. Beneath the frescoes are traces of a green textile design, which originally filled the lower part of the three frescoed walls. The scheme was completed by an altarpiece of the *Deposition*, which was noted by Vasari but has since disappeared. The idiom of the frescoes in the Vatican is strikingly different from that of the frescoes at San Marco. In wealth of detail and variety of incident, in richness of texture and complexity of grouping, they violate the canons of the earlier scenes. But if we had to reconstruct the probable appearance of a fresco by the author of the San Marco predella, our mental image would resemble the frescoes in the Vatican more closely than those in the convent cells. Not only was the style of the San Marco frescoes governed by considerations which did not apply to the frescoes in the Vatican, but the narrative problem of the Vatican frescoes was, of its very nature, more intimately linked with that of Angelico's predella panels than with that of the cells. Hence it is wrong to regard the discrepancy between the fresco cycles as a measure of Angelico's development. But within the Chapel there is evidence of stylistic change, and it is here that we must look for proof of the influence upon Angelico of his new environment. In the normal course the lunettes above would have been painted before the scenes below. The upper frescoes (Pls. 103–105) are divided vertically in the centre by a wall serving a dual function in relation to the two parts of the scene. Thus the raised platform on which the *Ordination of Saint Stephen* takes place is continued in the contiguous scene of *Saint Stephen distributing Alms*, the background of towers and houses in the *Saint Stephen preaching* is common also to the *Saint Stephen addressing the Council*, and a single strip of landscape unifies the *Expulsion of Saint Stephen* and the *Stoning of Saint Stephen*. This consecutive narrative has no counterpart in the lower cycle (Pls. 106–108), where each scene is independent of the next and the compositions are centralized. Whereas the loosely constructed upper scenes have something of the character of enlarged predella panels, the monumental scenes below establish a type of composition which remained constant in Florentine painting till the time of Ghirlandaio. The architectural setting plays a more important part in the lower frescoes than in those above, and in the finest of them (above all in the *Ordination of Saint Lawrence*, the *Saint Lawrence distributing the Treasures of the Church* and the *Saint Lawrence distributing*

13. THE CEILING OF THE CHAPEL OF NICHOLAS V. Vatican.

Alms) the individual figures have a new gravity and a new plastic emphasis. Vitiated as they are by their uneven execution (most clearly exemplified in the trivial subsidiary figures on each side of the Saint in the *Saint Lawrence distributing Alms*), these are the most ambitious and most fully developed of Angelico's large-scale designs. It is interesting to note that the *Martyrdom of Saint Lawrence* once more depends from a Trecento prototype, in this case a fresco by Bernardo Daddi in Santa Croce in Florence.

The factor of restoration makes it difficult to determine the exact extent of Angelico's responsibility for the two cycles. It has been suggested that the right half of the first and the whole of the third lunette were executed solely by assistants, and one student has gone so far as to deny Angelico's authorship of the cartoons of all of the six upper scenes. Both these views imply some measure of misunderstanding of the procedure by which the frescoes were produced. A document of 1447 records the names of the painters employed in the Chapel under the direction of Angelico. These are Benozzo Gozzoli, who received a higher salary than his companions and was evidently the master's chief assistant, Giovanni d'Antonio della Cecha, Carlo di ser Lazaro da Narni, and Giacomo d'Antonio da Poli. Three of these painters were again associated with Angelico at Orvieto, where one of them, Giovanni d'Antonio della Cecha, met with a fatal accident. Of the junior members of the studio we know nothing. But the senior member, Benozzo Gozzoli, has left us a dated work at Montefalco painted two years after the completion of the chapel in the Vatican. With a group of cognate works, this enables us to assess, at least approximately, his share in the Vatican frescoes. This was apparently limited to single heads and figures (three in the background of the first of the scenes from the life of St Stephen, three in the second, a number of the seated women in the third, two standing figures in the fourth, three figures in the fifth, and four heads in the sixth), and there is no case in which we would be justified in crediting Gozzoli with the whole of any scene. The three assistants paid at a lower rate would have been employed largely on the backgrounds and drapery, though one of them seems to have intervened from time to time in certain of the heads; this hand appears again in Cell 36 and the related frescoes at San Marco. The figure of the Saint is invariably by Angelico. As we would expect, the share of Angelico is greater in the lower and more visible than in the upper and less visible frescoes, and smallest in the relatively unimportant frescoes on the Chapel roof.

Beside the frescoes in the Vatican, the work completed by Angelico during his fourteen-week residence at Orvieto has attracted comparatively little interest. Engaged at the same salary as in the Vatican to paint for three months a year in the Cappella di San Brizio, where the miraculous corporal of the miracle of Bolsena was preserved, he filled two of the four triangular spaces on the ceiling of the chapel with a *Christ in Majesty with Angels* (Pl. 121) and *Sixteen Prophets* (Pl. 122). Angelico's part in these frescoes was smaller than in the Vatican, and seems to have been limited to the much damaged figure of Christ and a group of angels on the left of the first fresco and to the heads of a number of the seated prophets in the second. A receipt of September 1447 shows that the assistants engaged upon this work were the same as those employed in Rome. The fact that two spaces so large could be painted in three months and a half throws some light on the speed at which Angelico operated, and it is clear both in the Vatican and at Orvieto that the collaborative effort of his studio was the condition of his productivity. The contract for the frescoes must have been abrogated by 1449, when Gozzoli, who was working in Orvieto from July to December of this year, attempted to obtain the reversion of the commission. Forty years later Perugino was invited by the authorities of the Cathedral to complete the decoration of the Chapel, and in 1499 this was at length entrusted to Signorelli. Criticism has tended to concentrate unduly on the handling of the ceiling frescoes of Angelico, and to underrate their spacious compositions and their noble forms. But the contiguous vaults of Signorelli, so febrile and confused, suffice to prove how much posterity has lost through the failure of the master to complete two more of these superb designs.

In Rome Angelico received a salary of two hundred ducats a year. His principal assistant, Gozzoli, was paid at the rate of seven ducats a month, and Giovanni d'Antonio della Cecha and Giacomo d'Antonio da Poli were paid at the rate of two ducats and one ducat a month respectively. The total sum due to Angelico and his assistants in any period of twelve months was thus three hundred and twenty ducats. In the period between 1 January and 31 December 1449 payments to the studio amounted to no more than one hundred and eighty-two ducats, and it has been inferred from this that Angelico ceased work in Rome towards the end of July of this year. The post of Prior of San Domenico at Fiesole ran for a three-year term, and if elected in the summer of 1449 he would have remained as Prior at Fiesole until the summer of 1452. In practice the election perhaps took place earlier in the year, since in March 1452, when we next hear of him, Angelico, though resident at Fiesole, seems not to have been Prior of the convent. For nine years after the installation of the Dominican community at San Marco, the convents of San Marco and San Domenico were subordinated to a single Prior. This arrangement was terminated in 1445 by a bull of Eugenius IV, and following this Angelico's brother, Fra Benedetto, was elected Prior of the convent at Fiesole. As Sub-Prior of the joint convents under Sant'Antonino, Fra Benedetto seems to have continued the copying of choir-books and manuscripts for which he was so widely known, and there is no reason to suppose that Angelico's duties as Prior at Fiesole were so onerous as to compel him to discontinue painting. Two frescoes at San Marco, an *Annunciation* at the head of the staircase (Pls. 98, 101, 102) and a *Virgin and Child with Saints* in the corridor (Pls. 97, 99, 100), may have been executed after his return from Rome, since their main architectural features are common to the lower, and not the upper, cycle of frescoes in the Vatican. Both scenes belong with Angelico's panel paintings rather than with his frescoes, and form the climax respectively of the great *Annunciation* altarpieces that open with the painting at Cortona, and of the series of sacred conversations of which the San Marco, Annalena and Bosco ai Frati altarpieces are part. The change that had overtaken Angelico in Rome may be judged readily enough by comparing the first of the two frescoes with the *Annunciation* in Cell 3. As in the Chapel of Nicholas V, the figures are set on a diagonal axis and not on a single plane, and the robes of the angel and of the seated Virgin are correspondingly enriched. The colour is heavier than in the earlier scene, and the architectural setting assumes the same importance as the two protagonists. It has sometimes been suggested that this fresco is the work of an assistant; the placing of the figures in the picture space, however, speaks strongly against this view. The second fresco recalls the Bosco ai Frati altarpiece. Like the *Annunciation*, it reveals a greater measure of studio assistance than the autograph frescoes in the cells. But here again we find a new spaciousness in the design and a new equilibrium between the figures and their background which can only be explained if we assume that the fresco was preceded by that model of lucid narrative, the *Saint Lawrence receiving the Treasures of the Church*.

We learn from entries in the account books of the Cathedral of Prato that in the spring of 1452 Angelico was living at Fiesole, for on 21 March the Provveditore of the Duomo, Bernardo di Bandinello, came to Florence bearing a letter to Sant'Antonino which requested that 'frate Giovanni da Fiesole maestro di dipignere' should undertake the painting of the choir of the Cathedral. Eight days later Bernardo di Bandinello again visited Florence, this time to interview the painter and to persuade him to return to Prato to discuss the proposal with four deputies of the Cathedral and the Podestà. Presumably Angelico agreed to this, since on the following day horses were hired to take 'e Frate che dipigne' to Prato and back to Fiesole. For reasons we can no longer reconstruct, these conversations were inconclusive; on 1 April Angelico returned to Fiesole, and on 5 April Bernardo di Bandinello was once more in Florence, seeking a painter and a master of stained glass to decorate the choir. This time his search was successful, and the contract for the frescoes was awarded to Fra Filippo Lippi.

Among the few panel paintings that can be confidently ascribed to these years is a group of thirty-five scenes, designed to decorate the doors of the silver chest which stood in an oratory beside the chapel built by Michelozzo in the church of the Santissima Annunziata. On the strength of a passage in the chronicle of Benedetto Dei, these panels are thought to have been commissioned by Piero de' Medici at about the time of Angelico's return from Rome. They appear to have been left unfinished when Angelico went back to Rome (probably in 1452). A payment for the hinges of the chest in 1461, and another payment of 1462 show that work on the chest continued for over ten years. The panels show thirty-one scenes from the lives of Christ and the Virgin, opening with the *Annunciation* and closing with the *Coronation of the Virgin*, a *Last Judgment*, and two symbolical paintings at the beginning and end of the cycle. It has been suggested that the panels originally filled one single and a pair of double doors and the intervening space between them. If this is so, the single door must have been decorated with three rows of three panels, from the *Vision of Ezekiel* to *Christ teaching in the Temple*, the intervening space must have been filled with the *Marriage at Cana*, the *Baptism of Christ* and the *Transfiguration*, and the double doors must have contained the twenty-three scenes between *Christ carrying the Cross* and the double scene of the *Last Judgment*.

The panels are mentioned soon after 1460 by Fra Domenico da Corella in the *Theotocon* as works of Fra Angelico, and on this account alone it is difficult to follow the many critics who deny Angelico's intervention in, or general responsibility for, these little scenes. The attributional problem of the silver chest is essentially the same as that of the frescoes at San Marco. Like the San Marco frescoes, the paintings divide themselves into the two broad categories of panels designed by Angelico and executed by the master or his assistants, and panels designed and executed by other hands. All of the panels attributable to Angelico belong with those presumed to have constituted the first door. The three scenes which intervene between the doors are by Alesso Baldovinetti, and the remaining scenes are by a single hand which can be identified as that responsible for the fresco in Cell 2 and the cognate frescoes at San Marco. The compositions of these latter panels resemble Angelico's only in those cases where they incorporate motifs from the San Marco frescoes. This is the case with the *Mocking of Christ* (which depends from the corresponding fresco at San Marco), the *Christ carrying the Cross* (where the Virgin is based on the related figure in the fresco of this scene), and the *Coronation of the Virgin* (where the central group is a variant of that in Cell 9). The panels are not in a satisfactory state, though Ruskin exaggerates when he describes them as 'now in the most miserable condition, some two-thirds effaced, others so daubed and defaced as to alter the expression of the faces and make them monstrous or ludicrous'. In some cases subsequent retouching has robbed them of their vitality.

A cartellino appears at the top and bottom of each panel containing sentences respectively from the Old and the New Testament. Thus in the first scene Isaiah's prophecy of the Annunciation is balanced against the ECCE CONCIPIES IN VTERO ET PARIES FILIVM ET VOCABIS NOMEN EIVS IHESVM of St Luke, and in the sixth a passage from the Psalms, ELONGAVI FVGIENS ET MANSI IN SOLITVDINE, is accompanied by the words put by St Matthew into the mouth of the angel warning St Joseph to flee. The programme is relevant to Angelico in that it was almost certainly drawn up in its entirety before the panels were begun. A key to the conception is to be found in the first and last panels, one executed under the supervision of Angelico, the other by the artist who completed the chest. The first (Pl. 123) shows a landscape in the lower corners of which are the seated figures of Ezekiel and Gregory the Great. Between them flows the River Chobar, beside which Ezekiel received his vision of God. In the upper left corner are passages from the fourth, fifth and sixteenth verses of the first chapter of Ezekiel, describing the appearance of four 'animalia' and a wheel within a wheel. In the opposite corner is the gloss of St Gregory the Great upon this passage. The greater part of the panel is filled with two concentric circles, that in the centre containing eight standing figures of the Evangelists and writers of the canonical epistles, and that on the outside twelve figures of prophets. Round the perimeter of the smaller wheel run the opening words of the gospel of St John, and round the larger the account of the creation. The last panel shows a flowery field. On the left stands a female figure, the Church, holding a shield inscribed with the words LEX AMORIS. In the centre is a candlestick with seven branches through which are threaded seven scrolls. On each scroll is the name of a sacrament, accompanied to left and right by quotations from the Old and the New Testaments. From the middle of the candlestick rises a pennant, surrounded by a twisted scroll, and to right and left, supported by twelve apostles and twelve prophets, are the articles of the Creed and the passages from the Old Testament with which they were habitually juxtaposed. These two panels leave no doubt that the doors of the cupboard were designed as a profession of faith, and that their subject is the mystery of the Redemption, and not a mere sequence of New Testament scenes.

Though handling and condition are unequal, the first nine scenes are distinguished by exquisitely lucid schemes, in which the essence of Angelico's late style is distilled. The symmetrical architecture of the *Annunciation* (Pl. 124) (with its path running between two rows of cypresses and an open gateway that recalls the *Annunciation* of Domenico Veneziano), the charming *Nativity* (Pl. 125) (with its six adoring angels on the triangular stable roof and the rapt figures of the Virgin and St Joseph in a rectangle below), the *Circumcision* (Pl. 128) (where the vaulting reminds us of Domenico Veneziano's Santa Lucia altarpiece), the *Adoration of the Magi* (Pl. 129) (in which the diffuse scenes from the predellas of the Linaiuoli triptych and the Cortona *Annunciation* at last assume a perfectly coherent form), the much rubbed *Presentation in the Temple* (Pl. 127) (with its beautiful detail of the Child in profile at the base of a tall window in the centre of the scene), the *Flight into Egypt* (Pl. 126) (with its rolling landscape and its majestic figure of the Virgin on the ass), the *Massacre of the Innocents* (Pl. 131) (the only panel outside the San Marco predella in which Angelico portrays violent action, and the focus of some of the most remarkable deformations in his work), and the *Christ teaching in the Temple* (Pl. 130) (where the scene is punctuated by shafts of light falling behind the central figure and in the space between the arches on each side), all testify to an exceptional measure of inventiveness. Is it not possible that the popular estimate of these panels, with their happy union of formal sophistication and Lochner-like simplicity, shows a more real understanding of their value than the criticisms of students who have doubted their merits or questioned their authenticity?

After his term as Prior had expired, Angelico seems to have returned to Rome. From the time of the negotiations for the Prato frescoes till his death three years later, we have no reference to his activity, and we know only that before his death he was responsible for a further fresco cycle in the Vatican, that this can hardly have been begun before 1452, and that he died in Rome in 1455. There are two accounts of the *Scenes from the Life of Christ* painted by Angelico in the Chapel of the Sacrament in the Vatican. The fuller of these is a description by Vasari: 'He also did for the same Pope (Nicholas V) the chapel of the Sacrament in the Vatican palace, which was later destroyed by Paul III in order to put in a staircase. In this work, which was excellent, he painted in fresco in his own style some scenes from the life of Jesus Christ, in which he did many portraits from life of distinguished persons of those times. These would probably have been lost to-day had Giovio not saved them for his museum. They represent Pope Nicholas V, the Emperor Frederick, who came to Italy at that time, Fra Antonino, who was later Archbishop of Florence, Biondo da Forlì and Ferrante of Aragon.' According to the *Codice Magliabechiano*, the chapel was 'entirely painted by the hand of Fra Giovanni . . . the figures were painted with such grace and honesty that it was truly a paradise'. The Chapel of the Sacrament (alternatively known as the Chapel of St Nicholas) was rebuilt by Eugenius IV in 1433–4, and it is sometimes supposed that Angelico's *Scenes from the Life of Christ* were painted for this Pope before the frescoes in the secret chapel and the studio. The presence of a portrait of the Emperor Frederick III is, however, difficult to reconcile with so early a dating, since he did not visit Rome till March 1452, and there is thus a strong presumption that the frescoes were not begun before the summer of this year. The inclusion in

the frescoes of a portrait of Ferrante of Aragon is perhaps an indication that work upon them was continued after Angelico's death by Calixtus III, who was elected Pope on 8 April 1455. Portrait types were employed in the *Scenes from the Life of Saint Lawrence*, where, for example, the Pope in the fresco of *Saint Lawrence receiving the Treasures of the Church* is represented with the features of Pope Nicholas V, and their use in the Chapel of the Sacrament, though more general, was no more than an extension of the artist's practice in the earlier scenes. A drawing in the Louvre by an imitator of Angelico, showing *The Calling of Saints Peter and Andrew*, perhaps records the composition of one of the lost frescoes.

Vasari also mentions two other works executed by Angelico in Rome for the Dominican church of Santa Maria sopra Minerva. One of these was an altarpiece for the high altar, and the other was an *Annunciation* which in the middle of the sixteenth century hung on an adjacent wall. In the absence of these works an adventitious interest attaches to the only paintings by Angelico which appear to be later in date than the Annunziata silver chest, a triptych with the *Ascension, Last Judgment and Pentecost* in the Galleria Corsini in Rome (Fig. XXXII) and a *Christ on the Cross* in the Fogg Museum (Fig. 14). It is likely that the central panel of the Corsini triptych (Pl. 132) is autograph, and that the lateral panels derive from cartoons by Angelico. The closed, concentrated compositions are conceived in the same style as the scenes on the silver chest, and the figure of Christ, with right arm raised, is shown in the same pose as in the fresco at Orvieto. In the Christ of the *Ascension* we find the tendency to elongation that is evident in the Annunziata *Presentation in the Temple* and in other paintings of this time. This is apparent

14. CHRIST ON THE CROSS, WITH THE VIRGIN AND SAINT JOHN THE EVANGELIST, ADORED BY A DO- MINICAN CARDINAL. Fogg Museum of Art, Cambridge (Mass.).

also in the Virgin and St John of the picture in the Fogg Museum (Pl. 133). In this panel, as in so many of the earlier paintings of the theme, a figure kneels beneath the Cross. But it is characteristic of this last phase of Angelico's career that the kneeling figure is not St Peter Martyr or St Dominic, but the Dominican Cardinal Juan de Torquemada, whose scarlet hat rests on the ground beside a skull.

Angelico died on 18 March 1455, a few weeks before his patron Pope Nicholas V. His body was interred by his brethren in the north aisle of Santa Maria sopra Minerva, in a tomb (Fig. 15) bearing an inscription by the humanist Lorenzo Valla. This reads:

Here lies the venerable painter Fra Giovanni of the Order of Preachers.
Let me not be praised because I seemed another Apelles, but because I gave my riches, O Christ, to Thine.
For some works survive on earth and others in heaven. The city of Florence, flower of Etruria,
gave me, Giovanni, birth.
The glory, the mirror, the ornament of painters, Giovanni the Florentine is contained within this place.
A religious, he was a brother of the holy order of St Dominic, and was himself a true servant of God. His
disciples bewail the loss of so great a master, for who will find another brush like his? His fatherland and
order lament the death of a consummate painter, who had no equal in his art.

★   ★   ★

The five hundred years that have elapsed since the death of Fra Angelico have produced no artist with so universal an appeal. The *Annunciation* at Cortona, the *Deposition* from Santa Trinità, the frescoes at San Marco, the *Flight into Egypt* from the silver chest, all these form part of our common imaginative currency. Eschewing the personal mysticism, the private idiom of other great religious artists, they reflect the serenity, the discipline, the anonymity of communal religious life. In the case of Fra Angelico, more truly than in that of any other painter, the artist and the man are one. His paintings are informed with a tenderness, indeed affection, that gives tangible expression to the mystical virtue of charity, are undisturbed by profane interests and untinged by doubt. But an artistic reputation cannot rest on faith alone, and the appeal of Angelico's work is contingent not only on his sense of humility and awe in the divine presence, but on the incomparable visual sensibility by which this was transmitted, not only on his intellectual certainty, but on the solid forms and clear-cut compositions through which this was expressed.

In terms of the development of style, Angelico is a reactionary artist. Uninterested in the revolution in visual technique effected by his great contemporaries, save where this could contribute to expressiveness, he stands in opposition to the painting of his time. In the first half of the fifteenth century it is Angelico alone who deliberately reverts to models by Giotto and his followers, and even in his most progressive paintings, the frescoes in the Vatican, we are repeatedly reminded of the frescoed narratives of the Trecento. The language he employed resulted not from an involuntary failure to keep abreast of the developments of his own day, but from intentions which differed fundamentally from those of other artists. For all the translucent surface of his paintings, for all his rapturous pleasure in the natural world, there lay concealed, within Angelico's artistic personality, a Puritan faithful to his own intransigent ideal of reformed religious art. In the whole history of painting there are few instances of single-mindedness more notable than that with which Angelico pursued his path, and we can understand the style which he evolved, physically convincing yet devoid of sensuous appeal, direct, harmonious, elevated, only if we relate it to the moral system of which it was a visual counterpart.

15. THE TOMB OF FRA ANGELICO. Santa Maria sopra Minerva, Rome.

PLATES

1. CHRIST ON THE CROSS. San Domenico, Fiesole

2. VIRGIN AND CHILD ENTHRONED WITH TWELVE ANGELS. Staedel Institute, Frankfurt-am-Main

3. VIRGIN AND CHILD ENTHRONED WITH EIGHT ANGELS. Detail of Figure 1. San Domenico, Fiesole

4. SAINTS THOMAS AQUINAS AND BARNABAS. Detail of Figure 1. San Domenico, Fiesole

5. SAINTS DOMINIC AND PETER MARTYR. Detail of Figure 1. San Domenico, Fiesole

6. SAINTS AND BEATI OF THE DOMINICAN ORDER. Detail of Figure 1. National Gallery, London

7. SAINTS AND BEATI OF THE DOMINICAN ORDER. Detail of Figure 1. National Gallery, London

8. THE ANNUNCIATION. Museo del Gesù, Cortona

9. THE EXPULSION OF ADAM AND EVE. Detail of Plate 8

10. THE ANGEL OF THE ANNUNCIATION. Detail of Plate 8

11. THE VIRGIN ANNUNCIATE. Detail of Plate 8

12. THE MARRIAGE OF THE VIRGIN. Detail of Plate 8

13. THE VISITATION. Detail of Plate 8

14. THE ADORATION OF THE MAGI. Detail of Plate 8

15. THE PRESENTATION IN THE TEMPLE. Detail of Plate 8

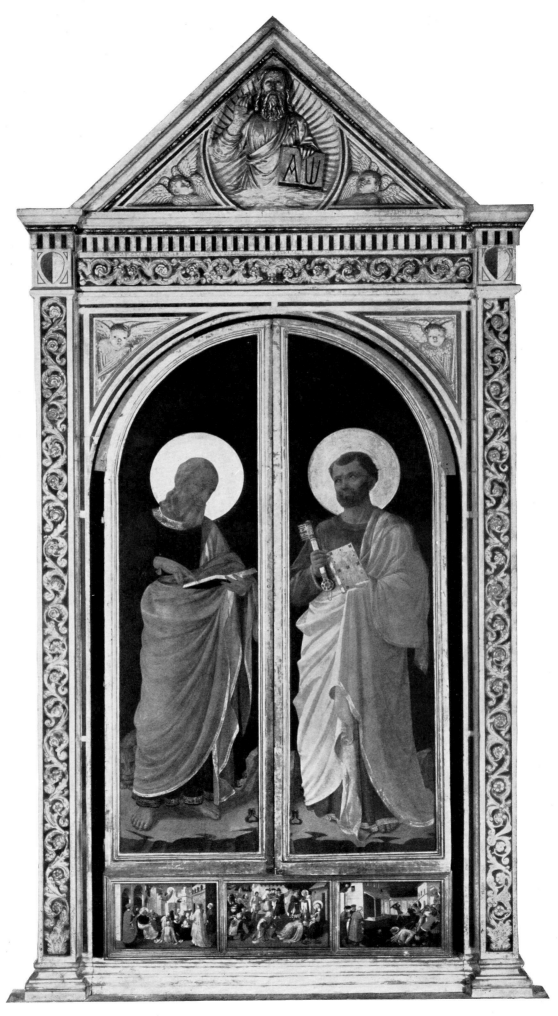

16a. THE LINAIUOLI TRIPTYCH (closed). Museo di San Marco, Florence

16b. THE LINAIUOLI TRIPTYCH (open). Museo di San Marco, Florence

17. SAINT JOHN THE EVANGELIST. Detail of Plate 16b

18. SAINT JOHN THE BAPTIST. Detail of Plate 16b

19-20. TWO ANGELS. Detail of Plate 16b

21–22. TWO ANGELS. Detail of Plate 16b

23. SAINT PETER PREACHING. Detail of Plate 16b

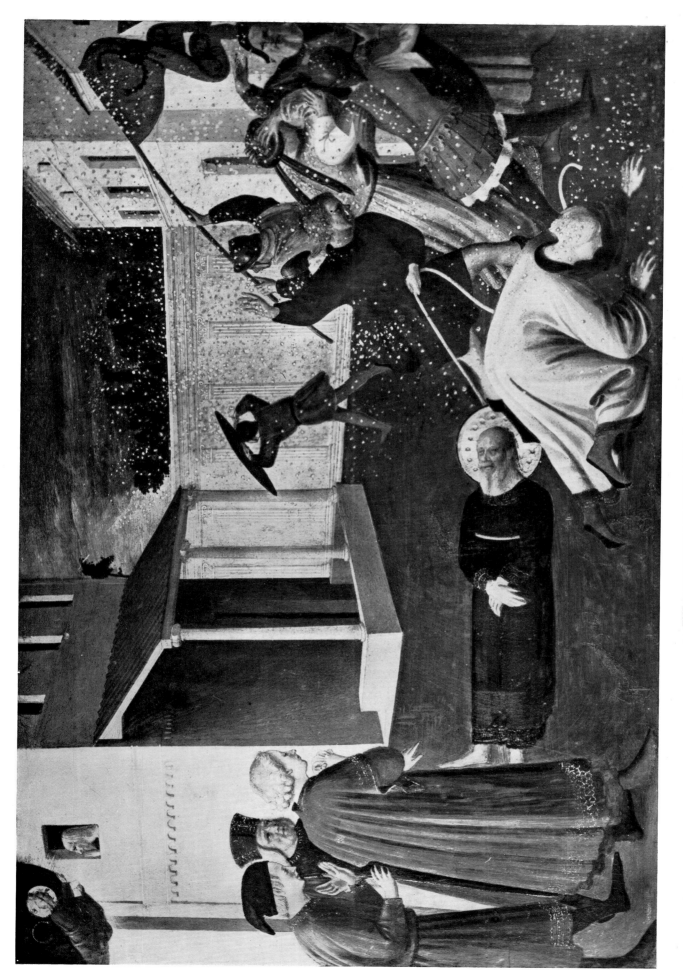

24. THE MARTYRDOM OF SAINT MARK. *Detail of Plate 16b*

25. VIRGIN AND CHILD BETWEEN SAINTS DOMINIC AND PETER MARTYR. San Domenico, Cortona

27. SAINT LUKE. Detail of Plate 25

26. SAINT JOHN THE EVANGELIST. Detail of Plate 25

28. SAINT JAMES THE GREAT FREEING HERMOGENES. Duc des Cars, Paris

THE NAMING OF SAINT JOHN THE BAPTIST. Museo di San Marco, Florence

29. THE NAMING OF SAINT JOHN THE BAPTIST. Museo di San Marco, Florence

30. VIRGIN AND CHILD ENTHRONED WITH FOUR ANGELS BETWEEN SAINTS MARK, JOHN THE BAPTIST, JOHN THE EVANGELIST AND MARY MAGDALEN. San Domenico, Cortona.

31. VIRGIN AND CHILD ENTHRONED WITH FOUR ANGELS BETWEEN SAINTS DOMINIC, NICHOLAS, JOHN THE BAPTIST, AND CATHERINE OF ALEXANDRIA.

Galleria Nazionale dell' Umbria, Perugia

32. SAINT JOHN THE EVANGELIST (underdrawing). Detail of Plate 30

33. SAINT JOHN THE BAPTIST (underdrawing). Detail of Plate 30

34. SAINTS DOMINIC AND NICHOLAS. Detail of Plate 31

35. SAINTS JOHN THE BAPTIST AND CATHERINE OF ALEXANDRIA. Detail of Plate 31

36. VIRGIN AND CHILD WITH SAINTS PETER MARTYR, COSMAS, DAMIAN, JOHN THE EVANGELIST, LAWRENCE AND FRANCIS.
Museo di San Marco, Florence

37. VIRGIN AND CHILD. Detail of Plate 36

38. THE CORONATION OF THE VIRGIN. Louvre, Paris

39. VIRGIN AND CHILD ENTHRONED WITH EIGHT ANGELS BETWEEN SAINTS LAWRENCE, JOHN THE EVANGELIST, MARK, COSMAS, DAMIAN, DOMINIC, FRANCIS AND PETER MARTYR. Museo di San Marco, Florence

40. SAINT COSMAS. Detail of Plate 39

41. SAINT DAMIAN. Detail of Plate 39

42. VIEW OVER WALL. Detail of Plate 39

43. VIEW OVER WALL. Detail of Plate 39

44. THE VIRGIN. Detail of Plate 38

FIVE SAINTS. Detail of Plate 38

45. THREE SAINTS. Detail of Plate 38

46. THE CRUCIFIXION OF SAINTS COSMAS AND DAMIAN. Alte Pinakothek, Munich

47. LYCIAS POSSESSED BY DEVILS. Alte Pinakothek, Munich

48. LYCIAS POSSESSED BY DEVILS. Detail of Plate 47

49. THE CRUCIFIXION OF SAINTS COSMAS AND DAMIAN. Detail of Plate 46

50. THE CRUCIFIXION OF SAINTS COSMAS AND DAMIAN. Detail of Plate 46

51. SAINTS COSMAS AND DAMIAN BEFORE LYCIAS. Alte Pinakothek, Munich

52. THE ATTEMPTED MARTYRDOM OF SAINTS COSMAS AND DAMIAN BY FIRE. National Gallery of Ireland, Dublin

53. THE BURIAL OF SAINTS COSMAS AND DAMIAN. Museo di San Marco, Florence

THE DECAPITATION OF SAINTS COSMAS AND DAMIAN. Louvre, Paris

54. THE DECAPITATION OF SAINTS COSMAS AND DAMIAN. *Louvre, Paris*

55. THE ENTOMBMENT. Alte Pinakothek, Munich

56. THE TEMPTATION OF SAINT ANTHONY THE ABBOT. Museum of Art, Houston

57. THE DEPOSITION. Museo di San Marco, Florence

58. HEAD OF CHRIST. Detail of Plate 57

59. SAINT MARY MAGDALEN. Detail of Plate 57.

60. A MALE HEAD. Detail of Plate 57

61. LANDSCAPE. Detail of Plate 57

ONLOOKERS AND DISTANT LANDSCAPE. Detail of Plate 57

62. LANDSCAPE. Detail of Plate 57

63. LANDSCAPE. Detail of Plate 57

64. LANDSCAPE. Detail of Plate 57

65. THE HOLY WOMEN. Detail of Plate 57

66. A GROUP OF ONLOOKERS. Detail of Plate 57

67. SAINT DOMINIC. Detail of Figure 11. Museo di San Marco, Florence

68. THE BEATA VILLANA AND SAINT CATHERINE OF ALEXANDRIA. Detail of Figure 11. Museo di San Marco, Florence

69. VIRGIN AND CHILD ENTHRONED WITH TWO ANGELS BETWEEN SAINTS ANTHONY OF PADUA, LOUIS, FRANCIS, COSMAS, DAMIAN AND PETER MARTYR. Museo di San Marco, Florence

70. VIRGIN AND CHILD. Uffizi, Florence

71. CHRIST ON THE CROSS ADORED BY SAINT DOMINIC. San Marco, Florence

72. SAINT DOMINIC. Detail of Plate 71

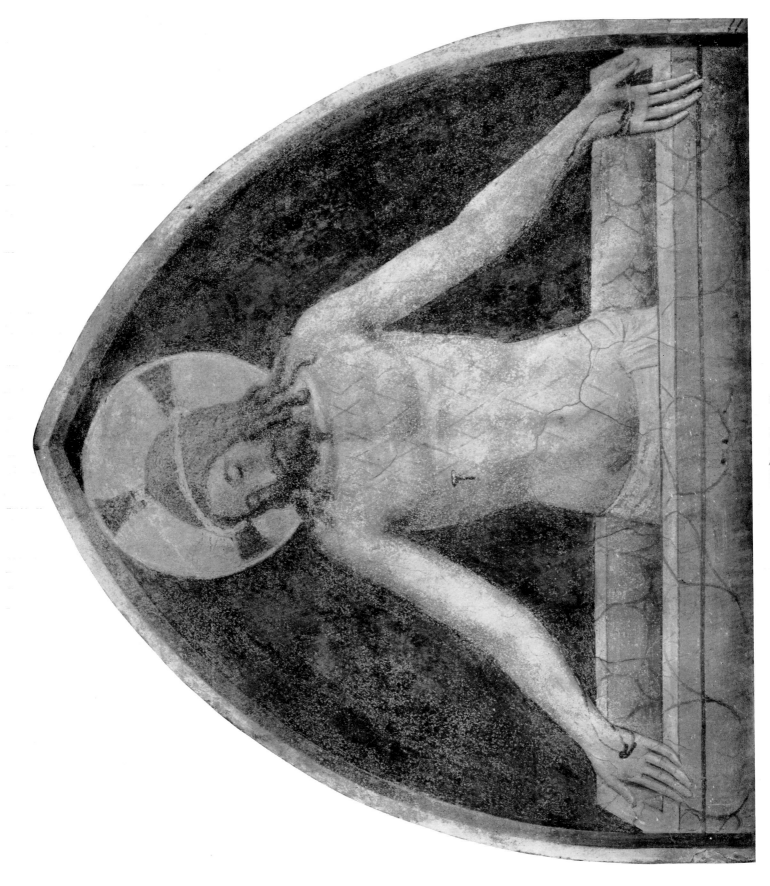

73. PIETÀ. San Marco, Florence

74. CHRIST AS PILGRIM RECEIVED BY TWO DOMINICANS. San Marco, Florence

75. SAINT THOMAS AQUINAS. San Marco, Florence

76. SAINT PETER MARTYR. San Marco, Florence

77. THE ADORATION OF THE MAGI. San Marco, Florence

78. THE CRUCIFIXION. San Marco, Florence

79. THE CRUCIFIXION. Detail of Plate 78

80. THE CRUCIFIXION. Detail of Plate 78

81. HEAD OF CHRIST. Detail of Plate 78

82. SAINT ANTONINUS. Detail of Plate 78

83. THE ANNUNCIATION. San Marco, Florence

84. NOLI ME TANGERE. San Marco, Florence

85. CHRIST. Detail of Plate 84

NOLI ME TANGERE. San Marco, Florence

86. THE VIRGIN ANNUNCIATE. Detail of Plate 83

87. THE MOCKING OF CHRIST. San Marco, Florence

88. CHRIST MOCKED. Detail of Plate 87

91. THE CORONATION OF THE VIRGIN. San Marco, Florence

92. THE CORONATION OF THE VIRGIN. Detail of Plate 91

93. THE TRANSFIGURATION. San Marco, Florence

THE TRANSFIGURED CHRIST. Detail of Plate 93

94. THE TRANSFIGURED CHRIST. Detail of Plate 93

95. MOSES. Detail of Plate 93

96. ELIAS. Detail of Plate 93

97. VIRGIN AND CHILD ENTHRONED WITH SAINTS DOMINIC, COSMAS, DAMIAN, MARK, JOHN THE EVANGELIST, THOMAS AQUINAS, LAWRENCE AND PETER MARTYR. San Marco, Florence

98. THE ANNUNCIATION. San Marco, Florence

99. SAINTS DOMINIC, COSMAS, DAMIAN AND MARK. Detail of Plate 97

100. THE CHRIST CHILD BLESSING. Detail of Plate 97

101. THE ANGEL OF THE ANNUNCIATION. Detail of Plate 98

102. THE VIRGIN ANNUNCIATE. Detail of Plate 98

102 THE ORDINATION OF SAINT STEPHEN, and SAINT STEPHEN DISTRIBUTING ALMS. Chapel of Nicholas V, Vatican

104. SAINT STEPHEN PREACHING, and SAINT STEPHEN ADDRESSING THE COUNCIL. Chapel of Nicholas V, Vatican

105. THE EXPULSION OF SAINT STEPHEN, and THE STONING OF SAINT STEPHEN. Chapel of Nicholas V, Vatican

106. THE ORDINATION OF SAINT LAWRENCE. Chapel of Nicholas V, Vatican

107. SAINT LAWRENCE RECEIVING THE TREASURES OF THE CHURCH, and SAINT LAWRENCE DISTRIBUTING ALMS. Chapel of Nicholas V, Vatican

108. SAINT LAWRENCE BEFORE DECIUS, and THE MARTYRDOM OF SAINT LAWRENCE. Chapel of Nicholas V, Vatican

109. SAINT STEPHEN AND SAINT PETER. Detail of Plate 103

110. SAINT STEPHEN GIVING ALMS. Detail of Plate 103

III. SAINT STEPHEN EXPELLED. Detail of Plate 105

112. SAINT STEPHEN PREACHING. Detail of Plate 104

113. A COUNCILLOR. Detail of Plate 104

114. SAINT JEROME. Detail of Figure XXVII

115. THE STONING OF SAINT STEPHEN. Detail of Plate 105

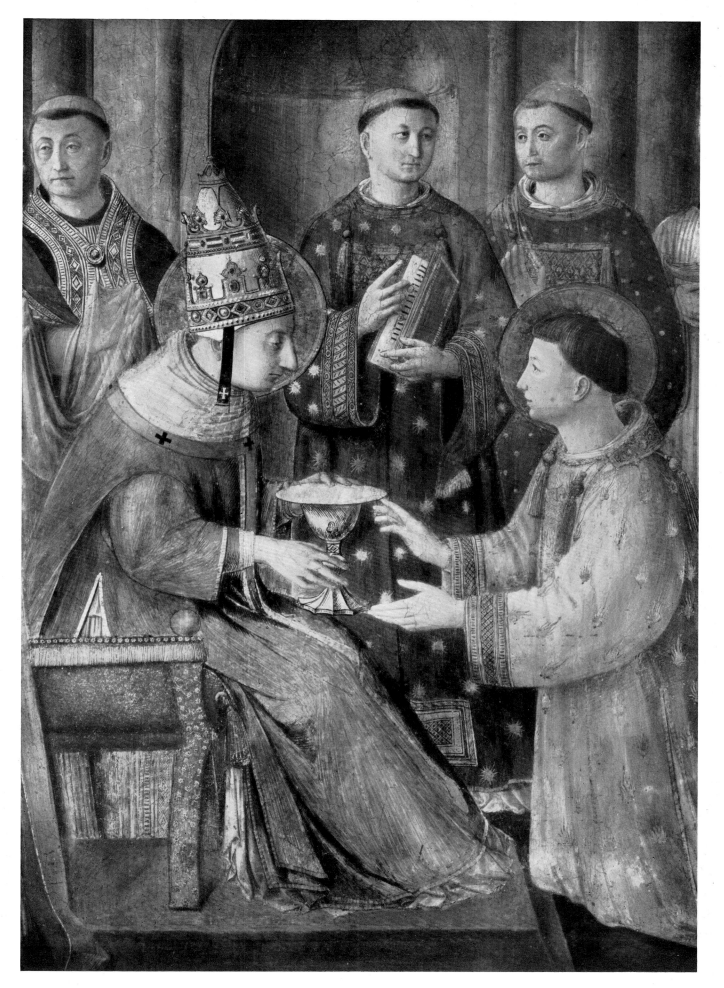

116. SAINT LAWRENCE AND THE POPE. Detail of Plate 106

117. SAINT LAWRENCE AND THE POPE. Detail of Plate 107

118. SAINT LAWRENCE BEFORE DECIUS, Detail of Plate 108

119. SAINT LAWRENCE GIVING ALMS. Detail of Plate 107

120. SAINT LAWRENCE IN HIS CELL. Detail of Plate 108

121. CHRIST IN GLORY. Duomo, Orvieto

PROPHETARVMLAVDABILISNVMERVS

122. PROPHETS. Duomo, Orvieto

123. THE VISION OF EZEKIEL. Museo di San Marco, Florence

ECCE CONCIPIES IN\VTERO 7 PARIES FILJVM 7 VOCABIS NOMEN EI IHESVM. LVCE 1. C

124. THE ANNUNCIATION (before restoration). Museo di San Marco, Florence

127. THE PRESENTATION IN THE TEMPLE. Museo di San Marco, Florence

CIRCVCIDIMINI DOMINO VIRI IVDA 7 AVFERTE PPVTIA CORDIVM VESTRVM . IER . IIII . C .

POSTQVAB CONSVMATI SVNT DIES OCTO VT CIRCVCIDERET PVER VOCATV E NOM EI IHES . LVCE . II . C .

128. THE CIRCUMCISION. Museo di San Marco, Florence

129. THE ADORATION OF THE MAGI (before restoration). Museo di San Marco, Florence

CÔFVSI SVT SAPIÊTES PTERRITI 7 CAPTI SVC SAPIÊSTIA NVLLA EST IN EIS .IERE.VIII.C

130. CHRIST TEACHING IN THE TEMPLE. Museo di San Marco, Florence

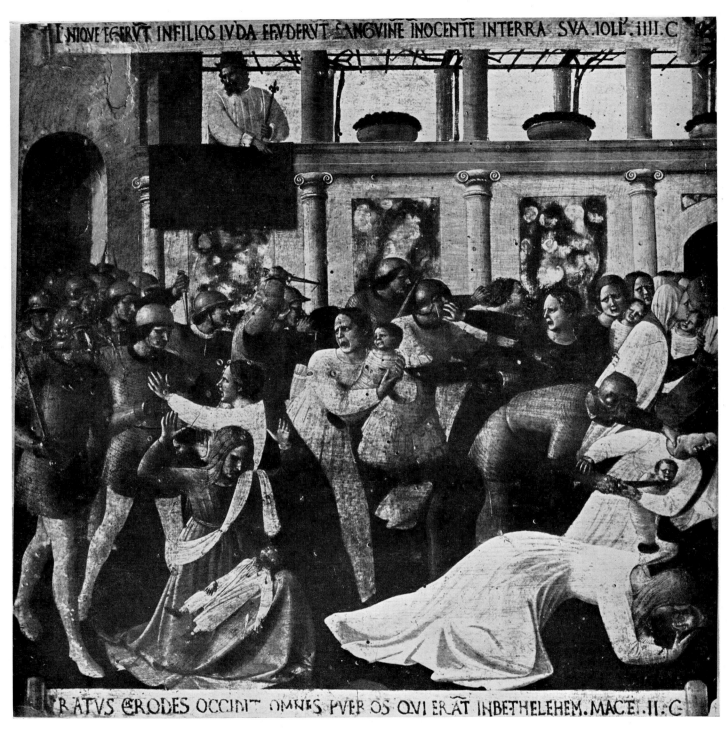

131. THE MASSACRE OF THE INNOCENTS (before restoration). Museo di San Marco, Florence

132. THE LAST JUDGMENT. Detail of Figure XXXII. Galleria Nazionale, Rome

133. CHRIST ON THE CROSS, WITH THE VIRGIN AND SAINT JOHN THE EVANGELIST, ADORED BY A DOMINICAN CARDINAL.
Detail of Figure 14. Fogg Museum of Art, Cambridge (Mass.)

CATALOGUE

ABBREVIATIONS

The following bibliographical abbreviations are employed throughout the notes:

BAZIN: Germain Bazin, *Fra Angelico*, English ed., Paris, 1949.

BEISSEL: Stephan Beissel, S.J., *Fra Giovanni Angelico da Fiesole, sein Leben und seine Werke*, Freiburg-im-Breisgau, 1905.

BERENSON 1896: Bernhard Berenson, *The Florentine Painters of the Renaissance*, New York, 1896.

BERENSON 1909: Bernhard Berenson, *The Florentine Painters of the Renaissance*, New York, 1909.

BERENSON 1932: Bernard Berenson, *Italian Pictures of the Renaissance*, Oxford, 1932.

BERENSON 1936: Bernard Berenson, *Pitture Italiane del Rinascimento*, Milan, 1936.

CODICE MAGLIABECHIANO: *Il Codice Magliabechiano*, herausgegeben von Carl Frey, 1892.

CROWE AND CAVALCASELLE: J. A. Crowe and G. B. Cavalcaselle, *A History of Painting in Italy*, edited by Langton Douglas and G. de Nicola, iv, London, 1911.

D'ANCONA: Paolo d'Ancona, 'Un ignoto collaboratore del Beato Angelico: Zanobi Strozzi', in *L'Arte*, xi, 1908.

DOUGLAS: Langton Douglas, *Fra Angelico*, London, 1900.

GAYE: Giovanni Gaye, *Carteggio inedito d'Artisti dei Secoli XIV, XV, XVI*, 3 vols., Florence, 1839–40.

GENGARO: Maria Luisa Gengaro, *Il Beato Angelico a San Marco*, Bergamo, 1944.

JAHN-RUSCONI: Arturo Jahn-Rusconi, *Il Museo di San Marco a Firenze*, Milan, 1950.

LIBRO DI ANTONIO BILLI: *Il Libro di Antonio Billi*, herausgegeben von Carl Frey, 1892.

LONGHI: Roberto Longhi, 'Fatti di Masolino e di Masaccio', in *La Critica d'Arte*, xxv–vi, 1940.

LONGHI 1928–9: Roberto Longhi, 'Un dipinto dell'Angelico a Livorno', in *Pinacoteca*, i, 1928–9.

MANETTI: 'Uomini singolari in Firenze del MCCCC inanzi,' in *Operette istoriche . . . di Antonio Manetti*, ed. Milanesi, Florence, 1887.

MARCHESE: P. Vincenzo Marchese, *Memorie dei più insigni Pittori, Scultori ed Architetti Domenicani*, 2nd ed., 2 vols., Florence, 1854.

MARCHESE 1853: P. Vincenzo Marchese, *San Marco Convento dei Padri Predicatori in Firenze, illustrato e inciso principalmente nei dipinti del B. Giovanni Angelico, con la vita dello stesso pittore e un sunto storico del Convento medesimo*, Florence, 1853.

VAN MARLE: Raimond van Marle, *The Development of the Italian Schools of Painting*, The Hague, x, 1928.

MURATOFF: Paul Muratoff, *Frate Angelico*, Italian ed., Rome, 1930.

PAATZ: Walter und Elizabeth Paatz, *Die Kirchen von Florenz*, Frankfurt-am-Main, i, 1940; ii, 1941; iii, 1952.

PAPINI: Roberto Papini, *Fra Giovanni Angelico*, Bologna, 1925.

RICHA: Giuseppe Richa, *Notizie Istoriche delle Chiese Fiorentine*, 10 vols., Florence, 1754–62.

SALMI 1950: Mario Salmi, 'Problemi dell'Angelico', in *Commentari*, i, 1950.

SCHOTTMÜLLER: Frieda Schottmüller, *Fra Angelico: des Meisters Gemälde*, Stuttgart, 1911.

SCHOTTMÜLLER 1924: Frieda Schottmüller, *Fra Angelico: des Meisters Gemälde*, 2nd ed., Stuttgart, 1924.

VASARI: *Le Vite de' più eccellenti Pittori, Scultori ed Architettori scritte da Giorgio Vasari pittore aretino*, con nuove annotazioni e commenti di Gaetano Milanesi, ii, Florence, 1906.

VENTURI: Adolfo Venturi, *Storia dell'Arte Italiana, VII: La Pittura del Quattrocento* i, Milan, 1911.

WINGENROTH: Max Wingenroth, *Angelico da Fiesole*, Leipzig, 1905.

WURM: Alois Wurm, *Meister- und Schülerarbeit in Fra Angelicos Werk*, Strassburg, 1907.

CATALOGUE

CHRIST ON THE CROSS. San Domenico, Fiesole.
Fresco: 363 × 212 cm.   PLATE 1.

Situated in the Sala del Capitolo of the convent, this fresco was covered with whitewash until 1882, and is not described by any early source. With the exception of Van Marle (x, p. 157), who regards it as a school work, the ascription to Angelico is admitted by all writers on the artist. An early dating (about 1420–30) is favoured by Schottmüller (1924, pp. 171, 265), a dating in the thirties by Douglas (pp. 82–3), and a dating about 1450 by Muratoff (p. 75). The fresco is evidently somewhat less mature than the two frescoes from San Domenico now at Paris and Leningrad (see below), and seems to date from about 1430.
The following frescoes also originate from San Domenico, Fiesole:

(i) CHRIST ON THE CROSS ADORED BY SAINT DOMINIC WITH THE VIRGIN AND SAINT JOHN. Louvre, Paris.
Fresco transferred to canvas: 435 × 260 cm.
Coll.: Bardini (1879).

The fresco was formerly in the refectory of San Domenico at Fiesole, where it is described by Marchese (i, pp. 232–3), who reports that it was then 'affatto perduto'. A passage in the *Chronaca Sancti Dominici de Fesulis* (f. 10), quoted by Marchese (loc. cit.), records that the fresco was restored by Francesco Mariani in 1566. Schottmüller (p. 267) regards the fresco as largely the work of an assistant. Light is thrown on the condition of the fresco by a photograph (Fig. 4) made while it was still *in situ* at Fiesole. This shows that the upper part of the fresco, above the arms of the Cross, has been made up, that the heads of the Virgin and St John have been reworked, and that the cloak of the Virgin and the habit of St Dominic (which were both extensively abraded) have been renewed. In their original form the heads of the three main figures are hardly consistent with a dating after 1433, and the fresco is thus of interest as offering a precedent for the similar frescoes executed in San Marco at Florence after 1438.

(ii) THE VIRGIN AND CHILD BETWEEN SAINTS DOMINIC AND THOMAS AQUINAS. Hermitage, Leningrad.
Fresco transferred to canvas: 196 × 187 cm.
Coll.: Capponi, Archduke Sergius of Russia (1882).

The fresco is described in the refectory (former Sala Capitolare) of San Domenico at Fiesole by Marchese (i, pp. 233–4), who notes that before removal from the convent wall it was extensively restored. Clumsy repainting is also noted by Milanesi (in Vasari, ii, p. 511 n.), and is confirmed by a photograph (Fig. 3) made of the fresco while it was still at Fiesole. Schottmüller (p. 261) proposes a dating about 1436. It seems likely, however, that before restoration the types of the two lateral Saints approximated to those of the Fiesole polyptych, and on this account the fresco, like that in the Louvre, must be dated before 1433.

A fresco of the *Virgin and Child* above the entrance to the church of San Domenico is listed in the *Codice Magliabechiano* (p. 95: 'Sono nella chiesa di San Domenicho di Fiesole piu tavole di sua mano, che molto bene per chj intende sono conosciute et maximo chj visto della maniera sua. Dipinse fuori sopra l'uscio di detta chiesa una Nostra Donna'). The fresco is referred to in the plural by Vasari (ii, pp. 512–3: 'Le pitture ancora che sono nell' arco sopra la porta di San Domenico, sono del medesimo'). These de-

scriptions suggest that the *Virgin and Child* must have formed the prototype for the external fresco above the doorway of San Domenico at Cortona. Paatz (ii, p. 5) assumes that the passage in Vasari refers to the Florentine church of San Domenico al Maglio.

THE VIRGIN AND CHILD ENTHRONED WITH TWELVE ANGELS. Staedelsches Kunstinstitut, Frankfurt-am-Main (No. 838).
Panel: 37 × 28 cm.   PLATE 2.

Purchased 1831 from Benucci. Schottmüller (p. 255) notes on the reverse of the panel the seals of the academies of Parma and Milan. The attribution of this panel to Angelico is accepted, *inter alios*, by Schottmüller (p. 3) and Van Marle (x, pp. 46–8) and, in part, by Berenson (1932, p. 22), and is denied by Muratoff (pp. 41–2). The angels surrounding the throne are so closely related to those in the Fiesole altarpiece as to be almost certainly by Angelico. Like the Fiesole altarpiece, the panel dates from about 1428. A coarse variant terminating in a pointed finial was formerly in the oratory of Sant' Ansano at Fiesole, and is now in the Museo Bandini (Fig. 1) (No. 11. Panel: 38 × 28 cm.). This is of interest as indicating the original form of the framing of the Frankfurt panel.

1. After FRA ANGELICO: VIRGIN AND CHILD ENTHRONED WITH TWELVE ANGELS. Museo Bandini, Fiesole.

THE VIRGIN AND CHILD ENTHRONED WITH
EIGHT ANGELS BETWEEN SAINTS THOMAS
AQUINAS, BARNABAS, DOMINIC AND PETER
MARTYR. San Domenico, Fiesole.

Panel: 212 × 237 cm.   PLATES 3–7. FIG. I.

The altarpiece is described by Vasari (ii, pp. 509–10): 'Dipinse,
similmente, a San Domenico di Fiesole la tavola dell'altar maggiore: la qual, perchè forse pareva che si guastasse, è stata ritoc-
cata da altri maestri e peggiorata. Ma la predella e il ciborio del
Sacramento sonosi meglio mantenuti; ed infinite figurine che in
una gloria celeste vi si veggiono, sono tanto belle, che paiono
veramente di paradiso, nè può chi vi si accosta saziarsi di vederle.'
A passage from the *Chronaca Sancti Dominici de Fesulis* (f. 5 t.),
transcribed by Marchese (i, p. 229 n.) and Giglioli (*Catalogo delle
cose d'arte e di antichità d'Italia: Fiesole*, 1933, pp. 24–5) shows that
the restoration of the painting was undertaken about 1501 by
Lorenzo di Credi: 'Circa anno Domini 1501, tempore prioratus
Fra Dominici de Mugello . . , renovata est tribuna capellae
majoris in duobus arcubus, et remotum est altare majus, et posi-
tum iuxta murum . . . et tabula altaris majoris renovata est et
reducta in quadrum et additae picturae, aer super picturas super-
ius et ornamenta tabulae per singularem pictorem Laurentium de
Credis.' The figure beside St Thomas Aquinas has been variously
identified as St John Evangelist (Milanesi, in Vasari, ii, p. 510 n.)
and St Peter (Marchese, loc. cit.), and seems to represent St
Barnabas (Schottmüller 1924, p. 256; Van Marle, x, p. 42), to
whom the high altar of the church was dedicated. In its original
form the altarpiece appears to have consisted, like that at Cortona, of three panels of approximately equal width, of which
that in the centre showed the Virgin and Child enthroned with
angels beneath a pointed arch, and those at the sides contained
two saints. The form of the pointed arch above the central group
and of the small arches above the lateral figures can still be seen on
the surface of the painting. As at Cortona, the figures were no doubt
originally set on a gold ground. In its present form, the throne
and baldacchino, the architectural setting and the landscape are
due to Credi, who was also responsible for repainting the heads of
the Saints Barnabas and Thomas Aquinas. The Virgin and Child,
the angels and the two Saints on the right are substantially by Fra
Angelico, whose hand is also evident in the Saints on the left side.
The earliest of Fra Angelico's surviving altarpieces, the painting
certainly precedes the *Madonna dei Linaiuoli* of 1432–3, and finds
a point of reference in the Todi *Madonna* of Masolino (1432), and
the somewhat earlier *Madonna* of Masolino from Santa Maria
Maggiore in Florence, formerly at Novoli. In view of these
analogies the painting may be tentatively dated about 1428–30.
The datings of Douglas (p. 82) in the bracket 1432–7 and of
Muratoff in the bracket 1418–20 are unacceptable.
Venturi (p. 40) points out that the present pilasters of the altarpiece (which are by Rossello di Jacopo Franchi) derive from
another painting. Moreni (*Notizie istoriche dei contorni di Firenze*,
iii, 1742, p. 90) and other writers ascribe the pilaster panels to
Lorenzo di Credi. It is not clear whether the reference is to the
original pilaster panels of Angelico (see below), to the present
pilasters, or to some intermediate figures by Credi, nor is it
certain at what date the substitution was made.
The predella described by Vasari (now replaced by a nineteenth-century copy) was purchased by a Florentine dealer
Metzger before 1827, and was later in the hands of V. Valentini,
Rome, and of A. MacBean, by whom it was sold (1860) to the
National Gallery, London (No. 663). It consists of five panels,

that in the centre (32 × 73 cm.) representing the Risen Christ
adored by angels, those to its left and right (32 × 64 cm. each)
two groups of Saints and Old Testament figures in adoration
headed respectively by the Virgin and by St John, and two
narrower outer panels (32 × 22 cm. each) with Saints and Beati
of the Dominican order (Fig. 1). The predella is accepted by
Douglas (p. 81), Wingenroth (p. 24), Berenson (1896, p. 100)
and other critics as wholly or partly by Angelico. Van Marle
(x, pp. 170–7), who gives the predella to Zanobi Strozzi, and
Muratoff (p. 31) deny the panels to Angelico, and presume that
they were executed a decade after the completion of the altarpiece. Against the view that the panels, like the pilasters of the
present altarpiece, were cannibalized from some other painting,
may be noted the fact that the dimensions of the three larger
panels correspond closely with those of the original upper panels
of the altarpiece, and that the poses of the angels in the centre of
the painting are connected with authentic early works of Fra
Angelico (e.g. the Frankfurt *Madonna*) and with the central
group of the present altarpiece. The whole of the central panel,
and the greater part of the panels to right and left, are, however,
the work of a studio assistant (probably Zanobi Strozzi). The
two outer panels, with Dominican Saints and Beati, which
would have stood beneath the pilasters of the altarpiece, are of
higher quality, and are largely autograph. A later copy of six
Old Testament figures from the inner right panel is in the Louvre
(No. 1294D). A detailed analysis of the iconography of the
predella is given by M. Davies (*National Gallery Catalogues: The
Earlier Italian Schools*, 1951, pp. 12–24).
The ciborium described by Vasari is tentatively identified by
Crowe and Cavalcaselle (iv, p. 88 n.) with a painted tabernacle
from the Stroganoff collection (Panel: 94 × 40 cm.; ex-Bardini,
Florence), now in the Hermitage at Leningrad; this is by the
same hand as the central panels of the predella in the National
Gallery. Two panels of Saints Mark and Matthew in the Musée
Condé, Chantilly (Nos. 4, 5. Panel: 36 × 11 cm.) are said to have
belonged to the pilasters of the altarpiece (Fig. II). These panels,
regarded as school works by Berenson (1932, p. 20), and ascribed
by Van Marle (x, pp. 184–5) to Zanobi Strozzi, are closely
related in style to the lateral Saints in the main panel, and are

II. FRA ANGELICO: SAINTS MARK AND MATTHEW.
Musée Condé, Chantilly.
SAINT NICHOLAS. Rev. A. Hawkins-Jones, Sheffield.

III. FRA ANGELICO: THE BIRTH OF SAINT DOMINIC
(detail of Plate 8).
Museo del Gesù, Cortona.

IV. FRA ANGELICO: SAINT DOMINIC RECEIVES
THE HABIT OF THE DOMINICAN ORDER (detail of
Plate 8). Museo del Gesù, Cortona.

autograph paintings by Angelico. Two similar autograph panels of Saints Nicholas and Michael (Panel: 36×14 cm. each) are owned by the Rev. A. Hawkins-Jones, Sheffield; these are stated in an inscription on the back to have formed part of a series of ten panels from an altarpiece in S. Domenico, Fiesole.

THE ANNUNCIATION. Museo del Gesù, Cortona.
Panel: 160 × 180 cm.   PLATES 8–15. FIGS. III, IV.
Painted for San Domenico, Cortona. Beneath the main panel is a predella showing: (i) *The Marriage of the Virgin*, (ii) *The Visitation*, (iii) *The Adoration of the Magi*, (iv) *The Presentation in the Temple*, and (v) *The Death of the Virgin;* at the outer edges are *The Birth of St Dominic* and *St Dominic receives the Habit of the Dominican Order*.
The Cortona *Annunciation* of Angelico is one of the most important archetypes in Florentine painting. Vasari (ii, p. 290) describes an *Annunciation* by Masaccio in San Niccolò oltr'Arno, 'nella quale, oltre la Nostra Donna che vi è dall'Angelo annunziata, vi è un casamento, pieno di colonne tirato in prospettiva, molto bello; perchè, oltre al disegno delle linee che è perfetto, lo fece di maniera con i colori sfuggire, che a poco a poco abbigliatamente si perde di vista; nel che mostrò assai d'intender la prospettiva.' It is possible, as Longhi (pp. 168, 187) suggests, that this lost painting was the source of the Cortona *Annunciation*. There is no documentary evidence for the date of the Cortona altarpiece. The datings proposed range from about

1424 (Douglas, in Crowe and Cavalcaselle, iv, 1911, p. 74 n.) to the late thirties (Van Marle, x, p. 70). The painting is assigned by Muratoff (p. 37) to the bracket 1428–30, by Bazin (p. 26) to the early thirties, and by Schottmüller (p. 258) to about 1435. The handling of perspective in the main panel and in the first and fourth panels of the predella is difficult to reconcile with the very early dating proposed by Douglas, and the scheme is, as a whole, more advanced than that of the Goldman *Annunciation* of Masolino (National Gallery of Art, Washington, No. 16) of about 1426. Within Angelico's work it was clearly produced after the Fiesole altarpiece and before the *Madonna dei Linaiuoli* of 1433. If, as is likely, it was painted about 1430, it would have preceded the altarpiece of the *Annunciation* painted by Angelico for Sant' Alessandro at Brescia in 1432, to which the following payments, transcribed by Marchese (i, pp. 349–50) refer:
'I°. 1432. Omissis aliis. 'Item la tavola della Nunziata fatta in Fiorenza, la quale depinse Fra Giovanni, ducatti nove. Item ducatti ij sono per oro per detta tavola, quali hebbe Fra Giovani – Giovanni de' Predicatori da Fiesole – per dipingere la taola.'
With the exception of Wurm (pp. 4–5), writers on Angelico are agreed in regarding the *Annunciation* as an autograph work of the highest quality. The two outer panels of the predella are coarser in execution than the five interior panels. The five interior panels are accepted by Van Marle (x, p. 72) as works by the artist. Schottmüller (loc. cit.) notes discrepancies in their quality, Muratoff (p. 38) limits Angelico's responsibility to the *Visitation*,

V. ZANOBI STROZZI: THE ANNUNCIATION.
San Francesco, Montecarlo.

Marriage of the Virgin and *Adoration of the Magi*, and Wurm (loc. cit.) reduces this still further to the single panel of *The Visitation*. Salmi ('Un ipotesi su Piero della Francesca', in *Arti Figurative*, iii, 1947, pp. 82–3) detects the hand of Piero della Francesca in the panel of *The Visitation*. All five scenes were certainly designed by Angelico, but the fifth, and perhaps also the fourth, show weaknesses of execution which seem to argue the intervention of a studio hand.

The *Annunciation* at Cortona formed the basis of a number of variants executed by imitators and by members of Angelico's studio. The most important of these are:

(i) THE ANNUNCIATION. San Francesco, Montecarlo.
FIG V.
Panel: (overall) 195×158 cm.; (main panels) 149×78 cm. each; (predella) 41×126 cm.

The altarpiece is wrongly supposed to have been transported to Montecarlo from the Franciscan church of Monte alle Croci outside Florence. In this event it would be identical with a painting recorded by Vasari (ii, p. 513): 'In San Francesco fuor della porta a San Miniato è una Nunziata.' If painted for Montecarlo, it cannot have been executed before 1438, when the church of San Francesco was still incomplete. The picture was certainly in the church in 1630, when it was restored by Pietro di Giovanni Renzi. The altarpiece is noted by Repetti (*Dizionario Geografico della Toscana*, iii, 1839, p. 334) as Sienese School, by Crowe and Cavalcaselle (iv, p. 76 n.), by whom it was incorrectly identified as a copy said to have been made of the *Annunciation* in San Domenico at Fiesole when this was removed to Spain in 1611, and by Magherini-Graziani ('Memorie e pitture di Masaccio in san Giovanni di Valdarno e nei dintorni', in the miscellaneous volume on *Masaccio*, 1904, pp. 92–4). A direct ascription to Angelico was proposed by Poggi ('L'Annunciazione del beato Angelico a San Francesco di Montecarlo', in *Rivista d'Arte*, 1909, vi, pp. 130–2), followed by Schottmüller (pp. 259–60), Van Marle (x, pp. 72–4), Procacci (*Mostra di opere d'arte trasportate a Firenze durante la guerra*, Florence, 1947, pp. 39–40) and Salmi (*Mostra d'arte sacra*, Arezzo, 1950, p. 96). The latter (1950, pp. 148–9) ascribes the predella to Battista di Biagio Sanguigni. The picture is regarded as a studio work by Berenson (1932, p. 22), Muratoff (p. 39) and Bazin (p. 181). The Montecarlo *Annunciation* differs from that at Cortona first in that the scene is split between two panels, secondly

in the illusionistic space architecture, thirdly in the poses of the two figures, which are greatly modified, and fourthly in its tonality, which is sharper and more astringent than that of the Cortona painting. The hand responsible for this altarpiece recurs again in a number of other panels, and is almost certainly that of Zanobi Strozzi. Muratoff assigns the painting to the early thirties, and Poggi (more plausibly) to the period of the San Marco frescoes. Some of the changes introduced into the composition are due to the influence of altarpieces painted by Fra Filippo Lippi about 1440, and a dating about 1445 is very probable. The predella shows: (i) *The Marriage of the Virgin* (cut down), (ii) *The Visitation*, (iii) *The Adoration of the Magi*, (iv) *The Presentation in the Temple*, and (v) *The Burial of the Virgin*. These scenes are weaker variants of the corresponding panels in the predella of the Cortona *Annunciation*.

(ii) THE ANNUNCIATION. Prado, Madrid (No. 15).
Panel: 194×194 cm.
FIG. VI.

From San Domenico at Fiesole, where it is described by Vasari (ii, p. 510): 'In una cappella della medesima chiesa è di sua mano, in una tavola, la Nostra Donna annunziata dall'Angelo Gabbriello, con un profilo di viso tanto devoto, delicato e ben fatto, che par veramente non da uomo, ma fatto in paradiso: e nel campo del paese è Adamo ed Eva, che furono cagione che della Vergine incarnasse il Redentore. Nella predella ancora sono alcune storiette bellissime.' The altarpiece was sold to Duke Mario Farnese on 28 February 1611 for 1,500 ducats, and replaced in 1615 by an *Annunciation* by Jacopo da Empoli (S. de Vries, 'Jacopo Chimenti da Empoli', in *Rivista d'Arte*, xv, 1933, p. 382). It subsequently passed to the Duque de Lerma, was installed in the church of the Dominicans at Valladolid, was later moved to the Monastero de las Descalzas Reales in Madrid, and in 1861 was transferred to the Prado. The appearance of the picture was much changed by over-drastic restoration in 1933–4, and earlier comments on the quality of the painting must be read with this fact in mind. The attribution to Angelico is admitted by Berenson (1896, p. 100), Douglas (pp. 61–2), Sanchez-Canton (*Museo del Prado: Catalogo de los Cuadros*, 1949, pp. 12–3) and Salmi (1950, p. 81), but rejected by Schottmüller (p. 258), Van Marle (x, pp. 178–81) and Collobi-Ragghianti ('Zanobi Strozzi', in *La Critica d'Arte*, xxxii, 1950, p. 458), who ascribe it to Zanobi Strozzi, and by most other critics. The composition of the main panel is closely related to that of the *Annunciation* fresco at San Marco. The predella shows: (i) *The Marriage of the Virgin*, (ii) *The Visitation*, (iii) *The Adoration of the Magi*, (iv) *The Presentation in the Temple*, and

VI. ZANOBI STROZZI: THE ANNUNCIATION.
Prado, Madrid.

(v) *The Burial of the Virgin.* The second and fourth scenes are loosely related to the corresponding scenes of the Montecarlo predella, while the third employs features from the *Adoration of the Magi* on the Annunziata silver chest. The Prado altarpiece appears somewhat later than the Montecarlo painting, and may have been produced about 1455. The two altarpieces are by the same hand.

(iii) THE ANNUNCIATION. National Gallery, London (No. 1406).
Panel: 103 × 142 cm.
Coll.: Woodburn (imported from Italy 1818; sale, London, 9 June, 1860, lot 72), Nieuwenhuys (sale, Brussels, 4 May, 1883, lot 5), Bourgeois (till 1894).

This picture is traditionally stated to be identical with the painting of the *Annunciation* noted by Vasari (ii, p. 513) in San Francesco fuori della Porta San Miniato as a work of Angelico. As noted by Davies (*National Gallery Catalogues: The Earlier Italian Schools*, 1951, pp. 26-7), the arms on the capitals of the two columns are those of the Lanfredini family. Since there is a Lanfredini chapel in the church of San Francesco, the identification with the painting in San Francesco described by Vasari is highly probable. The altar-piece, which is loosely dependent on the Montecarlo *Annunciation* and has been cut down, is given by Berenson (1932, p. 365) and Van Marle (x, pp. 190-2) to Domenico di Michelino. Collobi-Ragghianti ('Domenico di Michelino', in *La Critica d'Arte*, xxxi, 1950, p. 365) identifies a panel of the *Expulsion* in the Reber collection, Lausanne (80 × 56 cm.) as part of the missing left side of the altarpiece.

(iv) THE ANNUNCIATION. San Martino a Mensola, near Florence.
This painting, which derives from the Cortona *Annunciation*, is assigned by Muratoff to the school of Angelico in the bracket 1430-40, but can hardly have been painted before 1450. Berenson (1932, p. 348) ascribes it to an early phase of the Master of San Miniato.

THE LINAIUOLI TRIPTYCH. Museo di San Marco, Florence.   PLATES 16-24. FIG. 5, VII.
Panel: 260 × 330 cm.

Commissioned in 1433 for the guild-hall of the Arte dei Lin-aiuoli, the triptych shows: (*centre*) *The Virgin and Child enthroned*, in the frame twelve music-making angels, (*right*) *Saint John Evangelist*, (*left*) *Saint John Baptist*. On the outer faces of the wings are (*right*) *Saint Mark*, (*left*) *Saint Peter*. Beneath is a pre-della representing (*centre*) *The Adoration of the Magi*, (*left*) *Saint Peter preaching*, (*right*) *The Martyrdom of Saint Mark*.
A record of the commissioning of the altarpiece, contained in the *Libro dei Debitori e Creditori dell'Arte de' Linaiuoli* (c. 98 t.), is transcribed by Baldinucci (*Notizie de' Professori del Disegno*, iii, 1768, pp. 91-2) and more accurately by Gualandi (*Memorie originali italiane riguardanti le belle arti*, iv, 1843, p. 110):
MCCCCXXXIII a di II di luglio
(*in margine*) Dipintura del Tabernacolo a Frate Giovanni. Richordo chome detto di e sopradetti Operaj alogharono a frate Guido, vocato fre Giovanni delordine di Sto Domenicho da fiesole adipignere uno tabernacolo di nostra donna nella detta arte dipinto di dentro e di fuori, co Colori oro et azzurro et aricto, de migliori et piu fini che si truovino, con ogni sua arte et industria per tutto et per sua faticha et manifattura per Fior. 190 doro o quello meno che parra alla sua coscientia. Et co quelle figure che sono nel disegno chome di tucto appare alibro de partiti di detta arte segnato D a c. 214 Fior. 190.
The marble frame in which the triptych is set was designed by Ghiberti in 1432; documents of 29 October 1432 and 11 August 1433, printed by Gualandi (op. cit., pp. 109, 110-1), refer re-spectively to the execution of a wooden model by Jacopo di Piero detto il Papero, and to the commissioning of the tabernacle in its final form from two assistants of Ghiberti, Jacopo di

VII. FRA ANGELICO: THE LINAIUOLI TRIPTYCH (central panel before restoration). Museo di San Marco, Florence.

Bartolommeo da Settignano and Simone di Nanni da Fiesole. Analogies for the style of the four Saints in the wings are pre-sented by the wing of the Masaccio-Masolino triptych from Santa Maria Maggiore, Rome, now in the National Gallery.
A wide variety of view has been expressed as to the extent of studio intervention in the altarpiece; Schottmüller (pp. 257-8) regards the triptych as largely autograph, and Wurm (pp. 18-20) admits only the St Mark as the work of Fra Angelico. The Virgin and Child, some of the angels in the frame, and the four Saints in the wings appear to have been executed largely, if not wholly, by Angelico. The predella is ascribed to a studio assistant by Muratoff (p. 43). Van Marle (x, p. 60) makes an attempt to dis-sociate the outer panels from that in the centre, which he accepts as Fra Angelico's; no valid qualitative distinction can be drawn between the three panels. The view of Wurm (loc. cit.) that 'die Entwürfe für die drei Predellenbilder . . . sind nicht vom Meister' can be ruled out.
Old photographs leave no doubt that the central panel (Fig. VII) has been extensively restored, that the greater part of the Virgin's cloak is not original in its present form, and that the shape of the Virgin's head has been slightly modified. The angels in the frame have also been weakened by retouching. In the *Saint Peter preach-ing* the heads of the figure in profile on the right and of the two standing figures on the extreme left are much damaged by repaint.

A variant of the panel of *Saint Peter preaching*, formerly in the Nemes collection at Munich (sale catalogue, 1931, p. 19), published by L. Venturi (in *Pantheon*, 1928, p. 20) as Angelico, is by a studio hand.

THE VIRGIN AND CHILD WITH SAINTS DOMINIC AND PETER MARTYR. San Domenico, Cortona.

PLATES 25–27

The fresco, which must originally have shown the Virgin seated in full-length between kneeling figures of Saints Dominic and Peter Martyr, fills the lunette above the west door of San Domenico. In the interior of the pointed arch are four seated figures of the Evangelists. Despite their damaged state, both the main fresco and the subsidiary figures are clearly the work of Angelico. A bull issued by Eugenius IV in 1438, empowering the Prior of San Domenico to apply certain funds to the painting of the church, is not (as is supposed by Marchese, i, pp. 218–9) in itself evidence of the date at which the fresco was executed, and the cartoon of the central figure suggests that the lunette is probably contemporary with the polyptych inside the church.

SAINT JAMES THE GREAT FREEING HERMOGENES. Duc des Cars, Paris.

PLATE 28.

Panel: 26 × 24 cm.

See note on the following plate. The episode is described in the *Legenda Aurea*.

THE NAMING OF SAINT JOHN THE BAPTIST. Museo di San Marco, Florence.

PLATE 29.

Panel: 26 × 24 cm.

Along with two panels of *The Marriage of the Virgin* and *The Burial of the Virgin*, also in the Museo di San Marco, this panel was presumed by Crowe and Cavalcaselle (iv, p. 91) to have formed part of the predella of the Santa Maria Nuova *Coronation of the Virgin* in the Uffizi, with which it was at one time exhibited. The fact that the panels originate from two separate sources (the present painting was purchased in 1778 by Vincenzo Prati, while the supposed companion panels were presented to Cosimo II in 1629 and reached the Uffizi in 1704), and that their dimensions are incompatible (the two larger scenes measure 19 × 50 cm.) makes this conjunction improbable. Van Marle (x, pp. 181–2) ascribes *The Naming of the Baptist* (along with *The Marriage of the Virgin* and *The Burial of the Virgin*) to Zanobi Strozzi. Muratoff (p. 36) denies all three panels to Angelico. In style the present panel is related to the predella of the Linaiuoli triptych. As is pointed out by Salmi ('La giovinezza di Fra Filippo Lippi', in *Rivista d'Arte*, xviii, 1936, p. 9), the panel must date before 1435, since it forms the basis of a scene in the predella of the polyptych at Prato executed by Andrea di Giusto in this year. Longhi (p. 176) links the *Naming of the Baptist* with a panel of *Saint James freeing Hermogenes* (wrongly described as *Christ conferring the Power to bind and loose*), in the collection of the Duc des Cars, Paris. The identical heights of the two panels and their closely similar handling favour this grouping. Two panels of *The Nativity* and *The Agony in the Garden* in the Pinacoteca at Forlì (of the same height but considerably narrower) are regarded by Longhi as further fragments of the same predella; the different scale of the figures in these panels, and the fact that they cannot be ascribed to Angelico with any confidence, militate against this view. There is no indication of what altarpiece the San Marco and Des Cars panels formed part.

THE VIRGIN AND CHILD ENTHRONED BETWEEN SAINTS JOHN EVANGELIST, JOHN BAPTIST, MARK AND MARY MAGDALEN. San Domenico, Cortona.

PLATES 30, 32, 33. FIG. VIII.

Panel transferred: (central panel) 137 × 68 cm.; (lateral panels) 117 × 69 cm.

Painted for San Domenico, Cortona. In the finials are the Annunciatory Angel, Christ on the Cross between the Virgin and St John, and the Virgin Annunciate. The predella of the altarpiece, now in the Museo del Gesù, Cortona, shows (i) *The Dream of Honorius III and the Meeting of Saints Dominic and Francis*, (ii) *Saints Peter and Paul appearing to Saint Dominic*, (iii) *The Raising of Napoleone Orsini*, (iv) *The Disputation of Saint Dominic and the Miracle of the Book*, (v) *Saint Dominic and his Companions fed by Angels*, and (vi) *The Death of Saint Dominic*. The polyptych is identified by Douglas (pp. 66–7, 123) with a painting recorded as executed on the commission of Niccolò di Angelo Cecchi for the chapel of St Thomas Aquinas in San Domenico. It is, however, clear from a document of 1452 which alludes to this painting (Cortona, Archivio Communale, quoted by Douglas, loc. cit.) that the chapel of St Thomas Aquinas had a secondary dedication to St Nicholas of Bari, and in these circumstances the painting referred to is more probably the polyptych by Sassetta in the same church, in which this Saint is shown. The companion polyptych of Sassetta on the corresponding altar at the head of the left (north) aisle is related in form to the polyptych of Fra Angelico, and was perhaps executed about 1436. Douglas attaches to the polyptych of Fra Angelico the hypothetical date of 1437. Venturi (pp. 40–2) favours an earlier dating, and Muratoff (pp. 40–1) regards the altarpiece as closely linked in style with the *Annunciation* in the Gesù, and on these grounds dates it about 1430. Schottmüller (p. 259) proposes a dating between 1430 and 1440. Stylistically the altarpiece forms a middle term between the Linaiuoli triptych (1433) and the Perugia polyptych (1437). Wurm (pp. 15–6) admits only the head of St Matthew as autograph. The two outer figures are somewhat weaker than those in the interior of the wings, but the underdrawing of the figures (see below) indicates clearly that all of the main figures were sketched in by a single hand.

The action of damp, precipitated by conditions of storage in 1940–4, resulted in the rotting of the panels of the altarpiece and the disintegration of the gesso priming. In 1945–6 the film of the paint surface was removed from all five panels, and photographs of this taken from behind provide important evidence for the technical procedure which underlies Angelico's altarpieces (*Florence: Mostra di opere d'arte restaurate*, 1946, pp. 28–9, and Procacci, 'Recent Restoration in Florence II', in *Burlington Magazine*, lxxxix, 1947, pp. 330–1).

Iconographically the predella is closely related to that of the Louvre *Coronation of the Virgin*, of which it appears to have formed the prototype. The cartoons seem to be due to Angelico, and the execution to the hand responsible for the fresco in Cell 2 and other frescoes at San Marco.

THE VIRGIN AND CHILD ENTHRONED WITH ANGELS BETWEEN SAINTS DOMINIC, NICHOLAS OF BARI, JOHN BAPTIST AND CATHERINE OF ALEXANDRIA. Galleria Nazionale dell'Umbria, Perugia (No. 91).

PLATES 31, 34, 35. FIGS. 6–8.

Panel: (central panel) 130 × 77 cm.; (lateral panels) 95 × 73 cm.

Above the lateral panels are tondi of the Annunciatory Angel and the Virgin Annunciate. The pilasters contain twelve figures

VIIIA. MASTER OF CELL 2: THE DREAM OF HONORIUS III AND THE MEETING OF SAINTS DOMINIC AND FRANCIS; SAINTS PETER AND PAUL APPEARING TO SAINT DOMINIC. Museo del Gesù, Cortona.

VIIIB. MASTER OF CELL 2: THE RAISING OF NAPOLEONE ORSINI; THE DISPUTATION OF SAINT DOMINIC AND THE MIRACLE OF THE BOOK. Museo del Gesù, Cortona.

VIIIC. MASTER OF CELL 2: SAINT DOMINIC AND HIS COMPANIONS FED BY ANGELS; THE DEATH OF SAINT DOMINIC. Museo del Gesù, Cortona.

of Saints, arranged in three pairs on each side, of which those below are represented in full length and those above are cut off at the knee (*left side:* Saints Peter and Paul, Saints Benedict and Lawrence, Saints Mary of Egypt and Louis; *right side:* Saints John Evangelist and Stephen, Saints Peter Martyr and Thomas Aquinas, Saints Catherine of Siena and Jerome). The predella consists of three panels showing (i) *The Birth of Saint Nicholas, the Vocation of Saint Nicholas, and Saint Nicholas and the three Maidens*; (ii) *Saint Nicholas addressing an Imperial Emissary, and Saint Nicholas saving a Ship at Sea*; (iii) *Saint Nicholas saving three Men condemned to Execution, and the Death of Saint Nicholas.* Nos. (i) and (ii) are now in the Pinacoteca Vaticana (Nos. 251/2) and No. (iii) is in the Galleria Nazionale at Perugia (Panel: 33 × 63 cm. each).

Painted for the chapel of San Niccolò dei Guidalotti in San Domenico, Perugia, perhaps on the commission of the Bishop, Benedetto Guidalotti. A statement in the *Annali* of Padre Bottonio (MS., Bibl. Com., Perugia, ii, c. 72, quoted by Bombe, *Geschichte der Peruginer Malerei bis zu Perugino und Pinturicchio*, 1912, p. 77) ascribes the altarpiece to the year 1437: '1437. La tavola dell'Altare di S. Niccolo nella Cappella de' Guidalotti fu data questo anno a dipingere a F. Gio: da Fiesole padre nostro et famosissimo pittore de l'ordine nostro, di cui è ancora l'altra tavola posta in chiesa Vecchia sopra l'altar maggiore.' There is no record of a second altarpiece painted by Angelico for San Domenico at Perugia. The present painting was moved to the sacristy of the church before 1706. The triptych was disassembled before the middle of the nineteenth century (when the main panels were exhibited in the chapel of Santa Orsola in San Domenico, one of the predella panels hung above the door of the sacristy, and two more were already in the Vatican), and was reconstructed in 1915 (Cecchini, *La Galleria Nazionale dell'Umbria in Perugia*, 1932, pp. 13–6). The frame of the altarpiece is modern, and the reconstruction of the pilasters (which must originally have conformed to the double-sided pilasters of the *Deposition* in the Museo di San Marco) is incorrect. An accurate reconstruction appears in Bombe (op. cit., p. 79). A cleaning undertaken in 1918 appears to have involved extensive restoration, especially to the pilaster panels. The main panels of the altarpiece are substantially autograph, but in the central panel the Virgin's robe has been much retouched. The twelve pilaster panels (which are weaker than the corresponding panels of the *Deposition*) are by a single studio hand, as are the panels of the *Annunciation*. The three predella panels are ascribed by Weisbach (*Pesellino und die Romantik der Renaissance*, 1901, p. 38) to Pesellino, a view in which Schottmüller (p. 259) and Van Marle (x, pp. 66–8) seem to concur. Fra Angelico's responsibility for the predella panels is rightly accepted by Berenson (1896, p. 100), and by Venturi (p. 56), who exaggerates the part played by assistants in the main panels of the altarpiece.

THE VIRGIN AND CHILD ENTHRONED WITH SAINTS PETER MARTYR, COSMAS, DAMIAN, JOHN THE EVANGELIST, LAWRENCE AND FRANCIS. Museo di San Marco, Florence.
Panel: 180 × 202 cm.   PLATES 36, 37.

From the Dominican convent of San Vincenzo d'Annalena, Florence. The church of Annalena was not completed until 1453. There is, however, general agreement with the view of Schottmüller that Angelico's altarpiece was painted before this time, perhaps on the commission of the Medici, to whose family the foundress of the convent, Annalena Malatesta, was closely

linked. Crowe and Cavalcaselle (iv, 1911, p. 105 n.), followed by Van Marle (x, pp. 62–3), Muratoff (p. 45) and Jahn-Rusconi (Pl. 28) propose a dating in the thirties. The altarpiece is certainly later than the Linaiuoli triptych and the Cortona polyptych, and is somewhat less advanced in style than the San Marco altarpiece; it was perhaps produced about 1437–8. The surface of the panel has suffered from abrasion, but is otherwise relatively well preserved.

Beissel (p. 51) suggests that six scenes from the legend of Saints Cosmas and Damian, formerly in the Cappella di San Luca in the Santissima Annunziata, now in the Museo di San Marco, formed the predella of this altarpiece. These scenes (each of which measures 20 × 22 cm.) show: (i) *Saint Damian receiving Money from Palladia*, (ii) *Saints Cosmas and Damian and their Companions before the Judge*, (iii) *Saints Cosmas and Damian thrown into the Sea and rescued by an Angel*, (iv) *The attempted Martyrdom of Saints Cosmas and Damian by Fire*, (v) *The attempted Martyrdom of Saints Cosmas and Damian with Arrows*, and (vi) *The Decapitation of Saints Cosmas and Damian* (Fig. IX). If these panels formed the predella of the altarpiece, this must have contained two further scenes. On the analogy of the San Marco altarpiece, these are likely to have shown *The Burial of Saints Cosmas and Damian* and *The Dream of the Deacon Justinian*. The latter is almost certainly identical with a panel in the Spencer-Churchill collection, Northwick (Dimensions: 19.5 × 22 cm. Coll.: Duke of Lucca, sale, London, 1840, 25 July, lot 1). The attribution to Angelico of the six scenes at San Marco is accepted by Muratoff (p. 45) and, with reserve, by Berenson (1909, p. 105), and is rejected by Schottmüller (p. 237), Van Marle (x, p. 182), who ascribes the cycle to Zanobi Strozzi, and by Salmi (1950, p. 144), who assigns the execution of the first panel to Battista di Biagio Sanguigni and that of the remainder to Zanobi Strozzi. Paatz (i, p. 132) identifies them incorrectly as part of the San Marco altarpiece. The ascription to Angelico of the Spencer-Churchill panel is questioned by Phillips (in *Burlington Magazine*, xxxiv, 1919, p. 4) and Longhi (p. 175), who dates the panel before 1430 and detects the intervention of Andrea di Giusto. None of the panels is related compositionally to the corresponding scene of the predella of the San Marco altarpiece. The execution throughout the seven panels is due to Zanobi Strozzi.

IX. ZANOBI STROZZI: THE DECAPITATION OF SAINTS COSMAS AND DAMIAN. Museo di San Marco, Florence.

THE CORONATION OF THE VIRGIN. Louvre, Paris
(No. 1290).   PLATES 38, 44, 45.
Panel: 213 × 211 cm.

The altarpiece was painted for San Domenico at Fiesole, where
it was seen by Vasari (ii, pp. 510–11) on an altar to the left of the
church, and was transferred to Paris in 1812. Vasari's account
reads: 'Ma sopra tutte le cose fece Fra Giovanni, avanzò se
stesso, e mostrò la somma virtù sua e l'intelligenza dell'arte, in
una tavola che è nella medesima chiesa allato alla porta entrando
a man manca; nella quale Gesù Cristo incorona la Nostra Donna
in mezzo a un coro d'Angeli, e in fra una moltitudine infinita di
Santi e Sante, tanti in numero, tanto ben fatti, e con sì varie
attitudini e diverse arie di teste, che incredibile piacere e dolcezza
si sente in guardarle: anzi pare che que' spiriti beati non possino
essere in cielo altrimenti, o per meglio dire, se avessero corpi,
non potrebbono; perciocchè tutti i Santi e le Sante che vi sono,
non solo sono vivi e con arie delicate e dolci, ma tutto il colorito
di quell'opera par che sia di mano di un Santo, o d'un Angelo,
come sono: onde a gran ragione fu sempre chiamato questo
dabben religioso, Frate Giovanni Angelico. Nella predella poi,
le storie che vi sono della Nostra Donna e di San Domenico,
sono in quel genere divine; e io per me posso con verità
affermare, che non veggio mai questa opera che non mi paja
cosa nuova, ne me ne parto mai sazio.'

Beneath is a predella in seven compartments representing: (i)
The Dream of Pope Honorius III, (ii) *Saints Peter and Paul appearing
to Saint Dominic*, (iii) *The Raising of Napoleone Orsini*, (iv)
Pietà, (v) *The Disputation of Saint Dominic and the Miracle of the
Book*, (vi) *Saint Dominic and his Companions fed by Angels*, and
(vii) *The Death of Saint Dominic*.

The altarpiece was transported to Paris by Napoleon I in 1812,
and the predella, which had been separated from the upper panel,
was purchased in Florence in 1830. The pilasters and pinnacles
have disappeared. The iconography of the six narrative scenes
in the predella depends from the predella of the Cortona
polyptych.

A much damaged panel related in composition to the fourth
scene of the Louvre predella is in the collection of Sir Thomas
Barlow (Berenson, 'Quadri senza casa', in *Dedalo*, xii, 1932,
p. 528, as Fra Angelico), and a derivative from the third scene
was exhibited at Stuttgart in 1950 (*Frühe Italienische Tafelmalerei*,
No. 80, as by the Master of the Griggs *Crucifixion*).

The altarpiece is presumed by Douglas (p. 55) to have been
executed before 1430 on account of the Gothic form of the
throne. A dating about 1430 is proposed by Muratoff (pp. 41–2),
a dating after 1430 by Bazin (p. 26), and a dating between 1430
and 1440 by Schottmüller (p. 258). A measure of studio intervention is presumed by Papini (p. 39) and Muratoff (pl. xcix),
while Wurm (p. 10) regards the entire painting as a studio work,
and Salmi (1950, pp. 148–9) ascribes the kneeling Bishop in the
main panel to Battista di Biagio Sanguigni (b. 1392; d. after
1451). The main problem of the altarpiece arises from the employment in the upper panel of two different methods of space
representation. The first, characteristic of Angelico, is used for
the throne, tabernacle and steps; the second is employed in the
tiled pavement, and implies a fuller knowledge of the practice of
linear perspective than is evinced in any of the artist's other paintings. On this account it must be assumed that the altarpiece is by
two different hands, and was begun by Angelico and completed
by a younger artist. The predella, which employs the same
methods of perspective representation as the foreground of the
painting, is by the second hand. This analysis is confirmed by

X. ZANOBI STROZZI: THE CORONATION OF THE
VIRGIN. Uffizi, Florence.

examination of the heads, those of the standing figures to left and
right being, with one or two exceptions, characteristic of
Angelico, and those of the main group and of the foreground
figures by another artist. There are reasons for identifying this
second artist as Domenico Veneziano (Pope-Hennessy, 'The
Early Style of Domenico Veneziano', in *Burlington Magazine*,
xciii, 1951, pp. 216–23). Those parts of the altarpiece completed
by Angelico seem to have been painted before the San Marco
altarpiece of 1438–40, and the painting may thus have been
abandoned when work was begun on this painting and on the
frescoes in San Marco. The parts of the altarpiece executed by
Domenico Veneziano probably date from 1438 or 1439.

A reduced variant of the Louvre *Coronation of the Virgin* occurs
on one of three reliquary panels in the Museo di San Marco
(see p. 199), and another is found in a painting from Santa Maria
Nuova, now in the Uffizi (Fig. x. Panel: 112 × 114 cm.). The
latter is presumed to be identical with a painting noted by
Manetti (p. 166) and Vasari (ii, p. 516): 'Si vede anco nel tramezzo di Santa Maria Nuova una tavola di sua mano.' As pointed
out by Schottmüller (p. 257), the presence beside St Dominic of
Sant' Egidio (to whom the church of the hospital of Santa Maria
Nuova was dedicated) confirms this provenance. The Uffizi
Coronation omits the perspective features of the larger altarpiece
and abandons its spatial scheme in favour of a loosely organized
circular design. The picture is accepted as a work of Fra Angelico
by Berenson (1896, p. 98), Douglas (pp. 56–8) and Muratoff (pp.
32–3), who date it about 1425, and by Schottmüller (loc. cit.),
who places it in the bracket 1430–40. Van Marle (x, pp. 48–52)
detects the hand of Zanobi Strozzi in the main figures, and Bazin
(p. 181) regards it as a studio reduction after the Louvre altarpiece. If, as is likely, the painting depends from the Louvre
Coronation, it cannot have been produced before 1440. The hand
responsible for executing it is that tentatively identified as
Zanobi Strozzi's, and occurs again in the four reliquary panels
from Santa Maria Novella at San Marco and Boston, and in the
predella of *The Marriage and Burial of the Virgin* at San Marco (see
p. 170). The latter panels appear to have formed the predella of
the Santa Maria Nuova *Coronation*.

THE VIRGIN AND CHILD ENTHRONED WITH ANGELS WITH SAINTS COSMAS AND DAMIAN, LAWRENCE, JOHN EVANGELIST, MARK, DOMINIC, FRANCIS AND PETER MARTYR. Museo di San Marco, Florence.   PLATES 39–43.
Panel: 220 × 227 cm.

Painted for the high altar of San Marco, Florence. The altarpiece is described by Vasari (ii, pp. 508–9): 'Ma particolarmente è bella a maraviglia la tavola dell'altar maggiore di quella chiesa: perchè, oltre che la Madonna muove a divozione chi la guarda per la semplicità sua, e che i Santi che le sono intorno, sono simili a lei; la predella, nella quale sono storie del martirio di San Cosimo e Damiano e degli altri, è tanto ben fatta, che non è possibile immaginarsi di poter veder mai cosa fatta con più diligenza, nè le più delicate o meglio intese figurine di quelle.' In 1745 the altarpiece was noted by Richa (vii, p. 143) in a passage leading to the sacristy. The surface of the panel is much abraded, but is not disfigured by modern restoration.

There is no record of the commissioning of the altarpiece. The convent of San Marco was handed over to the Dominicans in 1436. In 1437 work was begun on the rebuilding of the convent proper and of the church, the roof of which was unsound. Structural work in the Cappella Maggiore of the church was completed in 1439, and its decoration is presumed to have been finished by Epiphany 1443, when it was dedicated, in the presence of Eugenius IV, by the Archbishop of Capua. In 1438 Cosimo de' Medici agreed to present to the convent of San Domenico at Cortona an altarpiece which had previously stood on the high altar of San Marco in Florence (Gaye, i, p. 140), and in 1440 this altarpiece (by Lorenzo di Niccolò) was installed at Cortona. A passage from the *Cronaca di San Marco* transcribed by Milanesi (in Vasari, ii, p. 534) confirms the details of this transaction. This reads in full (Raoul Morçay, *La cronaca del convento di San Marco*, 1913, p. 14): 'Tempore illo, fratre Cypriano existente adhuc Priore, tabula altaris majoris quae magna et pulchra erat, ornata multis figuris ac valoris ducatorum ducentorum vel circa, donata fuit a fratribus conventui Cortonii ordinis nostri, operante ad hoc praecipue fratre Cypriano antedicto; cui fecit apponere arma seu insignia Medicea et dictorum Medicorum nomina; necdum perfecta erat tabula quae nunc est super dictum altare majus.' There is thus a high degree of probability that the altarpiece painted by Angelico for the high altar of the church was commissioned in 1438 and completed in or soon after 1440.

Eight narrative panels are presumed to have formed part of the altarpiece. These are:

(i) *The Healing of Palladia by Saints Cosmas and Damian, and Saint Damian receiving a Gift from Palladia.* National Gallery of Art (Kress Collection), Washington (No. 790).   FIG. 9.
Panel: 36.5 × 47.5 cm.

Coll.: Keller, New York. The panel shows on the left the miraculous cure of Palladia by the two Saints, and on the right St Damian receiving a gift pressed on him by the grateful woman in the name of Christ.

(ii) *Saints Cosmas and Damian and their Brothers before Lycias.* Alte Pinakothek, Munich (No. H.G. 36).   PLATE 51.
Panel: 38 × 45 cm.

Purchased in 1822 from Weiss, Berlin, for the Bavarian Royal Collection. The panel shows the two Saints and their three brothers before the proconsul Lycias, who orders them to sacrifice to the pagan gods.

(iii) *Lycias possessed by Devils: Saints Cosmas and Damian thrown into the Sea.* Alte Pinakothek, Munich (No. H.G. 37).
Panel: 38 × 45 cm.   PLATES 47, 48.

Provenance as (ii). The panel shows in the background (right) the five brothers thrown into the sea, and (left) rescued by an angel. In the foreground is Lycias assailed by devils, who leave him in response to the Saints' prayers.

(iv) *The attempted Martyrdom of Saints Cosmas and Damian by Fire.* National Gallery of Ireland, Dublin (No. 242).   PLATE 52.
Panel: 37 × 46 cm.

Coll.: Lombardi-Baldi; Graham; purchased for the National Gallery of Ireland, 1886. The five brothers are seen unscathed in the centre of a pyre or furnace, while the flames destroy their executioners.

(v) *The Crucifixion of Saints Cosmas and Damian.* Alte Pinakothek, Munich (No. H.G. 38).   PLATES 46, 49, 50.
Panel: 38 × 46 cm.

Provenance as (ii). The two Saints, crucified, are assailed (centre) with stones and (right and left) with arrows, which return to strike the executioners.

(vi) *The Decapitation of Saints Cosmas and Damian.* Louvre, Paris (No. 1293).   PLATE 54.
Panel: 36 × 46 cm.

Coll.: Niccola Tachinardi; Valentini, Rome; Palazzo Imperiali, Rome; Timbal (purchased 1868); acquired by the Louvre, 1882. The panel shows the execution of the five brothers.

(vii) *The Burial of Saints Cosmas and Damian.* Museo di San Marco, Florence.   PLATE 53.
Panel: 37 × 45 cm.

The panel shows a camel enjoining that the bodies of Saints Cosmas and Damian (which were to be separated on account of a supposed disagreement between the brothers) should be buried side by side.

(viii) *The Dream of the Deacon Justinian.* Museo di San Marco, Florence.   FIG. 10.
Panel: 37 × 45 cm.

The panel shows the two Saints replacing the cancerous leg of Justinian the Deacon with the healthy leg of an Ethiopian buried in the cemetery of S. Pietro in Vincoli.

It has also been suggested that a *Lamentation over the Dead Christ* in the Alte Pinakothek at Munich (No. H.G. 38a, Plate 55) formed part of the predella. The connection of this scene (which measures 38 × 46 cm., and was acquired in 1818 independently of the three other panels in the Pinakothek) with the predella is denied by Schottmüller (p. 260). It is, however, reasonably certain that this panel is identified with a 'Deposizione di Croce' listed along with seven scenes from the legend of Saints Cosmas and Damian in the Farmacia of the convent of San Marco at the time of the suppression, and likely that it also formed one of the 'quattro quadretti dell'Angelico . . . ch'erano in San Marco, ora in Germania,' restored in 1817 in Florence by Luigi Scotti (Marchese, i, p. 249). Bazin (p. 183) dismisses the supposed connection between the predella panels and the upper panel, which he assigns to different phases of the artist's evolution; this view is untenable. The reconstruction of the altarpiece presents great difficulty, since the aggregate width of the narrative panels (412 cm.) is greatly in excess of the width of the upper panel (227 cm.). It has been variously claimed that the predella consisted of eight scenes (Muratoff and Van Marle), seven (Douglas), six (Bodkin) and five (Crowe and Cavalcaselle and Collobi-Ragghianti). The balance of probability is against the view that the predella exceeded the width of the upper panel, and its width can thus hardly have been greater than the overall length of five of the narrative scenes. Bodkin ('A Fra Angelico Predella', in *Burlington Magazine*, lviii, 1931, pp. 183–94) concludes that it was composed (from left to right) of the scenes numbered (ii), (iii), (iv), (v), (vi) and (vii) above. Collobi-Ragghianti ('Zanobi Strozzi', in *La Critica d'Arte*, xxxii, 1950, pp. 468–73), arguing from the presence of gilt Ionic columns at the edges of certain of the panels, believes it to have consisted of scenes (ii), (i), (iv), (vi) and (vii). Both reconstructions presuppose that the panels not included were omitted from the altarpiece. This thesis is unacceptable, and no reconstruction is admissible which does not explain the siting of all of the nine panels. No inference can be drawn from the presence of gilt pilasters, as these also occur on the Munich *Pietà*, and seem originally to have been common to the entire cycle. In reconstructing the altarpiece we must therefore presume either that it had two predellas of five panels each, one in front and the other behind, or alternatively that it had in front a double predella of ten panels; the former thesis is unlikely, since Vasari gives no indication that the altarpiece was painted on the back. Accepting the second alternative, it may be noted that one of the narrative panels, that in the National Gallery of Ireland, is, as observed by Phillips (*Burlington Magazine*, xxxiv, 1919, p. 210), centralized in composition, and probably occupied a central place in the predella. This is true also of the Munich *Pietà*. In the narrative of the Saints' lives the *Attempted Martyrdom by Fire* is preceded by the *Judgment* and *Exorcism* scenes, and followed by the *Stoning*, *Decapitation* and *Burial*. The posthumous *Miracle of the Moor's Leg* must have followed the *Burial* scene, and the missing tenth panel would thus have been paired with the *Healing of Palladia* on the left side of the altarpiece. The predella in its original form may thus have shown:

(Missing scene)	Exorcism	Martyrdom by Fire	Crucifixion	Burial
Healing of Palladia	Judgment	Pietà	Decapitation	Dream of Justinian

In favour of this reconstruction it may be noted that (i) the figures in the lower scenes are consistently on a slightly larger scale than those in the scenes above, and (ii) that there is (as Angelico's other narrative cycles would lead us to expect) a connection between the aperture in the right wall of the *Palladia* and the wall on the left of the *Judgment* scene, and between the sloping roofs on the right of the *Exorcism* and the left of the *Martyrdom by Fire*. There is a general correspondence between the two interiors at each end of the lower row of panels, and there may also have been some degree of correspondence between the terminal panels in the row above. Like the upper panel of the altarpiece, the scenes in the predella are autograph paintings by Angelico. Weisbach (*Pesellino und die Romantik der Renaissance*, 1901, pp. 37–43) presumes the intervention of Pesellino; there is no evidence of this. The name of Piero della Francesca has also been mentioned in connection with the panels.

XI. FRA ANGELICO: SAINT THOMAS AQUINAS.
Private Collection.

Three panels with single figures of Saints in the Lindenau Museum at Altenburg (No. 92. Dimensions: 39 × 14 cm.), purchased in Rome in 1844 and stated to have come from San Marco, and a fourth panel of St Thomas Aquinas from the same series in an Italian private collection (Fig. XI), perhaps formed part of the pilasters of the altarpiece.

THE TEMPTATION OF SAINT ANTHONY THE ABBOT. Museum of Fine Arts, Houston (Edith A. and Percy S. Straus Collection).   PLATE 56.

Panel: 19 × 28 cm.
Coll.: William IV of Prussia; Count von Ingenheim; A. S. Drey; K. W. Bachstitz; Percy S. Straus, New York.

The panel is given by Berenson (1932, p. 22) to Angelico, and by Offner ('The Straus Collection goes to Texas', in *Art News*, 1945, 15–31 May, pp. 22–3) to the workshop of Angelico. Offner notes that 'this ingenious conception emerges from the fancy of Fra Angelico, but the execution is as certainly due to a follower. For, although the forms derive from the master's stock, they want in the intimate signs of his own hand.' The forms are not morphologically related to those of any identified personality in Angelico's workshop, and judging from photographs alone, it is difficult to believe that the execution of the panel as well as its cartoon is not due to Angelico. The panel seems to date from about 1440. No other parts of the predella have been identified.

THE DEPOSITION FROM THE CROSS. Museo di San Marco, Florence.   PLATES 57–66.

Panel: 176 × 185 cm.

Painted for Santa Trinità, Florence. The altarpiece is described in the sacristy of the church by Manetti (p. 166) and in the *Libro di Antonio Billi* (p. 18: 'Et nella sagrestia di Santa Trinita la tauola, doue è disposto Christo di croce') and by Vasari (ii, p. 513: 'e in Santa Trinità, una tavola della Sagrestia, dove è un Deposto di Croce, nella quale mise tanta diligenza, che si può fra le migliori cose che mai facesse annoverare'). The figure of Nicodemus is stated by Vasari (ii, p. 450) to be a portrait of the architect Michelozzo: 'Il suo ritratto è di mano di Fra Giovanni nella sagrestia di Santa Trinità, nella figura d'un Nicodemo vecchio con un cappuccio in capo, che scende Cristo di croce.' Crowe and Cavalcaselle (iv, p. 89) suggest that Michelozzo is represented not in the Nicodemus, but in the male figure with a black headdress to the left of the Cross, on the ground that this is more readily consistent with Michelozzo's age at the time when the altarpiece is presumed to have been executed.

Beneath the three sections of the principal scene are the inscriptions: (*left*) PLANGENT EVM QVASI VNIGENITVM QVIA INOCENS, (*centre*) ESTIMATVS SVM CVM DESCENDENTIBVS IN LACVM, and (*right*) ECCE QVOMODO MORITVR IVSTVS ET NEMO PERCIPIT CORDE. These passages come respectively from Zacharias, xii, 10; Psalm 87, v. 5; and Resp. III, Noct. II, Sabb. Sanct. The iconography of the panel is discussed by Beissel (pp. 54–7). The three pinnacles of the altarpiece, representing the *Noli Me tangere*, *The Resurrection* and *The three Maries at the Sepulchre*, are by Lorenzo Monaco, and were therefore executed before 1425. The pilasters, which are painted on two sides, show, reading from top to bottom, figures of: (i) *outside left*, Saints John Baptist, Lawrence and Augustine; (ii) *inside left*, Saints Michael, Andrew and Francis; (iii) *inside right*, Saints Peter, Paul and Dominic, and (iv) *outside right*, Saints Stephen, Ambrose and Jerome. In addition each pilaster contains two medallions with heads of Prophets or Saints.

The altarpiece has been dated about 1425 (Van Marle, x, p. 53), on account of the three pinnacles by Lorenzo Monaco, about 1435 (Muratoff, pp. 48–9, and Schottmüller, p. xxii), between 1435 and 1440 (Perkins, *La Deposizione: Beato Angelico*, 1948, p. 4), and between 1441 and 1446 (Douglas, pp. 91–3). A dating about 1440 is consistent with the style of the painting. Douglas (loc. cit.) regards the pinnacles as accretions to the altarpiece. This view is incorrect, and the fact that Lorenzo Monaco was closely associated with Santa Trinità suggests that the altarpiece was left unfinished at his death in 1425 and was resumed by Fra Angelico at a considerably later date.

Some measure of studio intervention is presumed by Muratoff (loc. cit.), who attempts to connect it with an assistant supposedly employed on the predella of the San Marco altarpiece, by Bazin (p. 182), who ascribes the figures on the left to the author of the *Nativity* fresco in San Marco (Cell 5), and by Wurm (pp. 44–5), who limits Angelico's responsibility to the figure of Christ. The left side of the altarpiece (and particularly the figures of the kneeling women) is somewhat weaker than the centre and right, and was probably executed, under Angelico's supervision and from his cartoon, by the Master of Cell 2 at San Marco.

Throughout the panel there is much retouching of a local character, and the cloud forms appear in some cases to have been changed. The predella of the altarpiece has disappeared.

THE LAMENTATION OVER THE DEAD CHRIST. Museo di San Marco, Florence (No. 58).

Panel: 108 × 165 cm.   PLATES 67, 68. FIG. 11.

Painted for the Confraternità di S. Maria della Croce al Tempio and originally over an altar on the left of the church (Paatz, iii, p. 308). The panel passed to the Accademia on the suppression of the confraternity in 1786. The painting is described in the *Libro di Antonio Billi* of 1516–25/30 (p. 18: 'Una tauola nel Tempio, doue e Giesu morto et intorno uno coro delle Marie'), by Vasari (ii, p. 514: 'Per la Compagnia del Tempio di Firenze fece, in una tavola, un Cristo morto') and by Richa (ii, p. 132). In addition to the figures present at the Deposition, the panel includes (*left*) St Dominic and (*right*) St Catherine of Alexandria and the Beata Villana. Milanesi (in Vasari, ii, p. 512 n.) notes that the inclusion of the Beata Villana in this painting is due to the fact that the Compagnia del Tempio exercised certain rights over the relics of this Saint in Santa Maria Novella. The painting is much damaged, and part of the background is new. The part played by studio assistants in the execution of this painting is generally assumed to have been more extensive than in the *Deposition*. The painting seems to have been executed in part by the Master of Cell 2 at San Marco and to date from the bracket 1440–5. A trecento *Lamentation* by Niccolò di Tourmaso in the Congregazione della Carità at Parma presents close similarities to, and may have been the model for, this painting.

THE VIRGIN AND CHILD ENTHRONED WITH TWO ANGELS BETWEEN SAINTS ANTHONY OF PADUA, LOUIS OF TOULOUSE AND FRANCIS, AND SAINTS COSMAS, DAMIAN AND PETER MARTYR. Museo di San Marco, Florence.

Panel: 171 × 172 cm.   PLATE 69.

Painted for the high altar of the Franciscan Observant church of San Buonaventura at Bosco ai Frati on the commission of

XII

XIII

XIV

XV

XVI

XII. FRA ANGELICO (?): THE MEETING OF SAINTS FRANCIS AND DOMINIC. Kaiser Friedrich Museum, Berlin.
XIII. FRA ANGELICO (?): THE APPARITION OF SAINT FRANCIS AT ARLES. Kaiser Friedrich Museum, Berlin.
XIV. FRA ANGELICO: THE DEATH OF SAINT FRANCIS. Kaiser Friedrich Museum, Berlin.
XV. FRA ANGELICO: SAINT FRANCIS BEFORE THE SULTAN (before restoration). Lindenau Museum, Altenburg.
XVI. FRA ANGELICO (?): THE STIGMATISATION OF SAINT FRANCIS. Pinacoteca Vaticana.

Cosimo de' Medici, whose villa at Cafaggiolo was not far distant from the convent and who was responsible for the rebuilding of the church (completed by Michelozzo in 1438). The *Chronaca del Chiostro di San Francesco in Mugello* of Fra Giuliano Ughi (Florence, Archivio di Stato, Storie e Relazioni miscellanee, vol. 167 nuovo, published by Fabriczy, 'Michelozzo di Bartolommeo', in *Jahrbuch der Preussischen Kunstsammlungen*, xxv, 1904, pp. 70–1), after describing the chalices, missals and vestments presented to the community by Cosimo de' Medici, adds: 'La bella tavola dell'altar maggiore, la quale dipinse un frate di S. Domenico.' The painting is more advanced in style than the San Marco altarpiece, and was probably executed in the bracket 1440–5. Some measure of studio intervention in the execution of the painting must be presumed. Bazin (p. 184) attempts to identify Angelico's assistant in this altarpiece as Benozzo Gozzoli. Apart from abrasion, the panel is relatively well preserved.

It is suggested by Schottmüller (p. 265) that the present predella (which shows the Pietà with Saints Peter, Paul, Bernardino and three other Saints) is an accretion to the altarpiece, and that this was originally completed by a series of scenes from the life of St Francis. These comprise:

(i) *The Meeting of Saints Francis and Dominic*. Kaiser Friedrich Museum, Berlin (No. 61).   FIG. XII.

Panel: 26 × 31 cm. Purchased 1823.

(ii) *The Apparition of Saint Francis at Arles*. Kaiser Friedrich Museum, Berlin (No. 62).   FIG. XIII.

Panel: 26 × 31 cm. Purchased 1823.

(iii) *The Death of Saint Francis*. Kaiser Friedrich Museum, Berlin (No. 61A).   FIG. XIV.

Panel: 29 × 70.3 cm. Coll.: Farrer; Fuller Maitland; purchased 1909.

(iv) *Saint Francis before the Sultan*. Lindenau Museum, Altenburg (No. 91).   FIG. XV.

Panel: 27   31 cm. Purchased in Rome 1845.

(v) *The Stigmatization of Saint Francis*. Vatican Gallery (No. 258).

Panel: 28 × 33 cm.   FIG. XVI.

The total width of these five panels is 196 cm. (or approximately 210 cm. when allowance is made for interstices between the panels). Collobi-Ragghianti ('Zanobi Strozzi', in *La Critica d'Arte*, xxxii, 1950, p. 467) suggests that the predella originates from the same altarpiece as the Pontassieve *Madonna*, now in the Uffizi; there is no evidence of this. The predella was almost certainly painted in the bracket 1440–5. Most critics are agreed that the execution of the panels is to a greater or lesser degree due to an assistant. The three panels at Berlin are so heavily restored that no verdict on authorship can be given in their present state. A photograph of the Altenburg panel before restoration leaves little room for doubt that this panel was at that time a damaged autograph work by Angelico. The cartoon of the panel in the Vatican, and perhaps also the execution, is Angelico's. Angelico is probably also to be credited with the cartoons of scenes (i), (ii) and (iii), the latter of which is based on the fresco of the same subject by Giotto in the Bardi Chapel, and seems, in the handling both of figures and architecture, to reveal the influence of Domenico Veneziano's predella to the *Coronation of the Virgin* in the Louvre. Scene (i) forms the basis of a fresco by Benozzo Gozzoli at Montefalco (1452), and it is not

XVII. FRA ANGELICO (?): SAINT FRANCIS.
John G. Johnson Art Collection, Philadelphia.

impossible that, if freed of restoration, this scene might prove to be an early work by Gozzoli.

THE VIRGIN AND CHILD. Uffizi, Florence.

Panel: 134 × 59 cm.   PLATE 70.

From the Prepositura di S. Michele Arcangelo, Pontassieve. On the frame at the base of the panel is an incomplete inscription which reads: TONIO DI LVCA E PIERO DI NICHOLAIO E SER PIERO (presumably with reference to the donors or the Operaii of the church). The panel, which evidently formed the centrepiece of a dismembered polyptych, was published for the first time in 1930, when it was shown at the Exhibition of Italian Art at the Royal Academy in London (No. 82). The picture is listed by Berenson (1932, p. 20) as a school work. Collobi-Ragghianti ('Zanobi Strozzi', in *La Critica d'Arte*, xxxii, 1950, p. 467) identifies a fragmentary *Saint Francis* in the Johnson collection, Philadelphia (Fig. XVII), as one of the missing lateral panels of the altarpiece, which she assigns to the bracket 1447–53. On grounds of style a dating about 1440–5 is not improbable. The Johnson panel (Panel: 59 × 41 cm.) is accepted as a work of Angelico by Schottmüller (p. 267, dated 1440–5) and Berenson (*Catalogue of the John G. Johnson Collection, Philadelphia*, i, 1913, pp. 10–11, No. 64, dated 1445–50), but can hardly have formed part of a polyptych, and perhaps originates from a lost *Crucifixion* by, or from the studio of, Angelico, analogous to that in S. Niccolò, Florence, wrongly associated with Angelico by Schottmüller (p. 225).

FRESCOES. San Marco, Florence.   PLATES 71–102.
The fifteenth-century frescoes in the convent of San Marco (most of which have at one time or another passed under the name of Fra Angelico) fall into four main groups:

(i) a *Christ on the Cross adored by Saint Dominic* and five lunettes of *Saint Dominic*, *Saint Peter Martyr*, *Saint Thomas Aquinas*, the *Pietà* and *Christ as Pilgrim received by two Dominicans* in the cloister.

(ii) a *Crucifixion with attendant Saints* in the Sala del Capitolo opening off the cloister.

(iii) a *Christ on the Cross adored by Saint Dominic*, an *Annunciation* and a *Virgin and Child with eight Saints* in the corridor on the upper floor.

(iv) forty-one frescoes in the forty-five cells on the upper floor.

The earliest reference to the frescoes at San Marco occurs in the *Cronaca di San Marco* of Fra Giuliano Lappacini (d. 1458). This reads: 'Tertium insigne apparet in picturis. Nam tabula altaris majoris et figurae capituli et ipsius primi claustri et omnium cellarum superiorum et Cruxifixi refectorii omnes pictae sunt per quemdam fratrem ordinis Praedictorum et conventus Fesulani qui habebatur pro summo magistro in arte pictoria in Italia, qui frater Johannes Petri de Mugello dicebatur, homo totius modestiae et vitae religiosae.' (Raoul Morçay, *La cronaca del convento di San Marco*, 1913, p. 16). The frescoes are also mentioned in the *Memoriale* of Albertini of 1510 (*Memoriale di molte statue e pitture della citta di Firenze fatto da Francesco Albertini prete*, Florence, 1863, p. 12: 'Nel magno convento et chiesa di Sancto Marcho, facto la maior parte dalla casa de' Medici, vi sono assai cose buone. La tavola maiore et il capitulo et le figure del primo claustro, per mano di frate Iohanni Ord. Pred.'), in the *Libro di Antonio Billi* of 1516–25/30 (p. 19: 'et il capitolo di Santo Marcho di Firenze et la tauola dello altare maggiore con piu altre fiure nella decta chiesa'), in the *Codice Magliabechiano* (p. 94: 'In Firenze nel monasterio de fratj di San Marcho dipinse il capitolo. E di sua mano nella chiesa de dettj fratj la tauola dell'altare maggiore. Et sono piu pitture di suo nel couento de dettj fratj'), and by Manetti (p. 166).

The extent of Angelico's responsibility for these frescoes, and particularly for the frescoes in the cells has been widely discussed. The views of the principal students of the artist are shown in the table on p. 181. There is no documentary evidence of the names or number of assistants employed in Angelico's studio in the years in which the frescoes were produced. The following notes refer to individual frescoes:

Cloister

CHRIST ON THE CROSS ADORED BY SAINT DOMINIC. (Plates 71, 72.) Dimensions: 340 × 155 cm. Described by Vasari (ii, p. 508): 'Fece poi nel primo chiostro, sopra certi mezzi tondi, molte figure a fresco bellissime, ed un Crucifisso con san Domenico a' piedi, molto lodato.' This much repainted fresco, which confronts the visitor as he enters the cloister of the convent, was designed and executed by Angelico. The visual effect is greatly impaired by a marble border of irregular shape added in 1628 (Paatz, iii, p. 32), after the cloister walls had been decorated by Poccetti and other artists. The original arched top of the fresco can be discerned below the marble frame. A weak variant of the composition in the upper corridor is framed in a painted rectangle. The background, the haloes and the black habit of St Dominic have been extensively retouched.

SAINT DOMINIC. The fresco occupies the lunette above the entrance to the Sala del Capitolo on the north side of the cloister. The surface is much abraded, but the placing of the figure on its ground leaves little doubt that it was executed by Angelico.

SAINT PETER MARTYR ENJOINING SILENCE. (Plate 76.) The fresco occupies the lunette above the entrance to the sacristy on the west wall of the cloister. The figure, though abraded, is less gravely damaged than the St Dominic, and was certainly executed by Angelico.

SAINT THOMAS AQUINAS. (Plate 75.) The fresco occupies the lunette above a door to the right of the entrance on the south wall of the cloister. Like the St Peter Martyr, to which its condition approximates, the figure was certainly painted by Angelico.

PIETÀ. (Plate 73.) The fresco occupies the lunette above the entrance to the antichamber of the refectory. Despite surface damage, this noble figure, with its bold triangular design, is one of the finest of the cloister lunettes.

CHRIST AS PILGRIM RECEIVED BY TWO DOMINICANS. (Plate 74.) The fresco occupies the lunette above the entrance to the hospice on the south side of the cloister. Though much damaged, the lunette, like the *Pietà*, was executed by Angelico. Beissel (p. 22) interprets the scene as an injunction to the friars that they should welcome guests with the same solicitude with which the pilgrims at Emmaus welcomed Christ.

Sala del Capitolo.

THE CRUCIFIXION WITH ATTENDANT SAINTS. (Plates 78–82.) Dimensions: 550 × 950 cm. The fresco, which occupies the north wall of the chapter house, is described by Vasari (ii, pp. 507–8): 'Fu questo Padre per i meriti suoi in modo amato da Cosimo de' Medici, che avendo egli fatto murare la chiesa e convento di San Marco, gli fece dipingere in una faccia del capitolo tutta la passione di Gesù Cristo; e dall'un de' lati tutti i Santi che sono stati capi e fondatori di religioni, mesti e piangenti a piè della croce; e dall'altro un San Marco Evangelista intorno alla Madre del figliuol di Dio venutasi meno nel vedere il Salvatore del mondo crucifisso; intorno alla quale sono le Marie che tutte dolenti la sostengono, e i Santi Cosimo e Damiano. Dicesi che nella figura di San Cosimo, Fra Giovanni retrasse di naturale Nanni d'Antonio di Banco, scultore ed amico suo. Di sotto a questa opera fece, in un fregio sopra la spalliera, un albero che ha San Domencio a' piedi; ed in certi tondi che circondano i rami, tutti i papi, cardinali, vescovi, santi e maestri di teologia, che aveva avuto insino allora la religione sua de' Frati Predicatori. Nella quale opera, aiutandolo i Frati con mandare per essi in diversi luoghi, fece molti ritratti di naturale, che furono questi: San Domenico in mezzo, che tiene i rami dell'albero; papa Innocenzio V francese; il beato Ugone, primo cardinale di quell'ordine; il beato Paulo fiorentino, patriarca; Sant' Antonino, arcivescovo fiorentino; il beato Giordano tedesco, secondo generale di quell'ordine; il beato Niccolò; il beato Remigio fiorentino; Boninsegno fiorentino, martire; a tutti questi sono a man destra: a sinistra poi Benedetto XI, trivisano; Giandomenico, cardinale fiorentino; Pietro da Palude, patriarca ierosolimitano; Alberto Magno, tedesco; il beato Raimondo di Catalogna, terzo generale dell'ordine; il beato Chiaro fiorentino, provinciale romano; san Vincenzio di Valenza, e il beato Bernardo fiorentino; le quali tutte teste sono veramente graziose e molto belle.' There is no reason to doubt Vasari's assurance that many of the heads of Dominicans beneath the main scene derive

PLAN OF THE CONVENT OF SAN MARCO
UPPER FLOOR

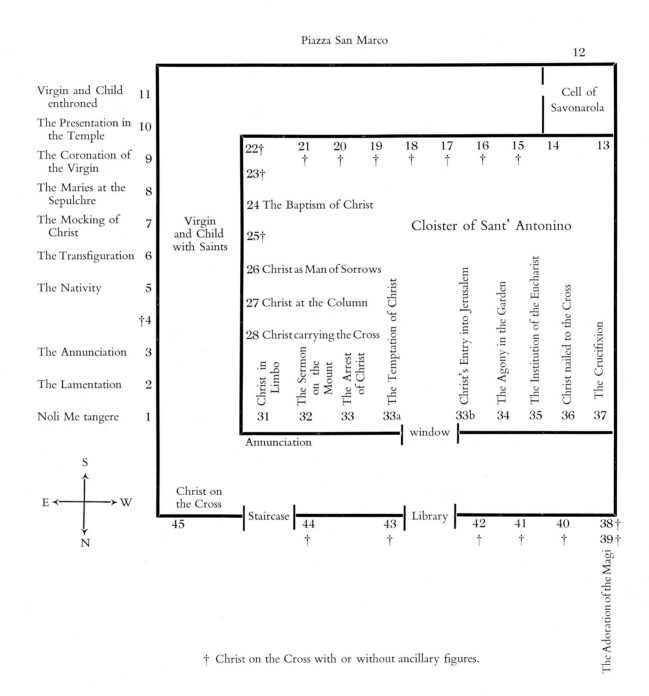

Piazza San Marco

12

Virgin and Child enthroned 11

The Presentation in the Temple 10

The Coronation of the Virgin 9

The Maries at the Sepulchre 8

The Mocking of Christ 7

The Transfiguration 6

The Nativity 5

†4

The Annunciation 3

The Lamentation 2

Noli Me tangere 1

Cell of Savonarola

22†   21   20   19   18   17   16   15   14   13
        †   †   †   †   †   †   †

23†

24 The Baptism of Christ

25†   Cloister of Sant' Antonino

26 Christ as Man of Sorrows

27 Christ at the Column

28 Christ carrying the Cross

Virgin and Child with Saints

Christ in Limbo | The Sermon on the Mount | The Arrest of Christ | The Temptation of Christ | Christ's Entry into Jerusalem | The Agony in the Garden | The Institution of the Eucharist | Christ nailed to the Cross | The Crucifixion

31   32   33   33a   33b   34   35   36   37

window

Annunciation

S
E ← → W
N

Christ on the Cross

Staircase   44   43   Library   42   41   40   38†
             †   †   †   †   †   39†

45

The Adoration of the Magi

† Christ on the Cross with or without ancillary figures.

XVIII. PLAN OF THE CELLS IN THE CONVENT OF SAN MARCO.

FRESCOES AT SAN MARCO: ANALYSIS OF ATTRIBUTIONS

	Subject	Berenson (1896)	Douglas	Schottmüller	Venturi	Van Marle	Muratoff	Bazin
Ground Floor Cloister:	CHRIST ON CROSS	A.	A.	A.	A.	A.	A.	A.
	ST DOMINIC	A.	A.	A.	—	A.	A. (?)	—
	ST PETER MARTYR	A.	A.	A.	—	A.	A. (?)	—
	ST THOMAS AQUINAS	A.	A.	A.	—	A. (r.)	A. (?)	—
	PIETA	A.	A.	A.	—	A.	A. (?)	—
	CHRIST AS PILGRIM	A.	A.	A.	—	A. (r.)	A. (?)	—
Sala del Capitolo:	CRUCIFIXION	A.	A.	A.	A.	A.	A. (p.)	A. (Ass. Master of *Nativity*)
Upper Floor Corridor:	CHRIST ON CROSS	A.	A.	Ass. (cartoon (by A.)	—	A. (r.)	A. (r.)	A. (p.)
	ANNUNCIATION	A.	A.	A.	A.	A.	Ass.	Master of *Annunciation* A. (p.)
	VIRGIN AND CHILD WITH SAINTS	A.	A.	A. (p.)	A.	A. (p.)	A.	(Ass. Master of *Annunciation*)
Cell No.								
1.	NOLI ME TANGERE	A.	A.	A.	—	Ass.	Ass.	Master of *Annunciation*
2.	LAMENTATION	A.	A.	A. (p.)	Ass. No. 1	Ass. (?)	Ass.	Master of *Nativity*
3.	ANNUNCIATION	A.	A.	A.	A.	A.	A.	A.
4.	CHRIST ON CROSS	A.	A. (r.)	Ass.	—	Ass.	Ass.	—
5.	NATIVITY	A.	A.	Ass.	Ass. No. 1	Ass.	Ass.	Master of *Nativity*
6.	TRANSFIGURATION	A.	A.	A.	A.	A.	A.	A.
7.	MOCKING OF CHRIST	A.	A.	A.	Ass. No. 1	A. (?)	A.	A.
8.	MARIES AT SEPULCHRE	A.	A.	A. (g.p.)	—	Ass.	Ass.	Masters of *Nativity* and *Annunciation*
9.	CORONATION	A.	A.	A.	A.	A. (p.)	A.	A.
10.	PRESENTATION	A.	A.	A. (? r.)	—	A. (r.)	A. (r.)	A.
11.	VIRGIN AND CHILD	A.	Ass.	Ass.	—	Ass.	Ass.	Master of *Nativity*
15–23.	CHRIST ON CROSS	A. (r.)	—	—	—	—	—	—
24.	BAPTISM OF CHRIST	A.	Ass. (cartoon by A.)	Ass.	Ass. No. 2	Ass.	Ass.	—
25.	CHRIST ON CROSS	A.	Ass.	Ass.	Ass. No. 2	A. (p.)	Ass.	—
26.	MAN OF SORROWS	A.	Ass. (cartoon by A.)	Ass.	Ass. No. 2	A. (p.)	Ass.	—
27.	FLAGELLATION	—	Ass.	—	—	Ass.	Ass.	—
28.	CHRIST CARRYING CROSS	A.	Ass. (cartoon by A.)	—	—	A.	Ass.	—
31.	CHRIST IN LIMBO	A.	A. (g.p.)	? Strozzi	—	Ass.	Ass.	—
32.	SERMON ON MOUNT	A.	A. (g.p.)	? Strozzi	—	A. (g.p.)	Ass.	—
33.	ARREST OF CHRIST	A.	A. (g.p.)	? Strozzi	—	Ass.	Ass.	—
33A.	TEMPTATION	A.	A. (g.p.)	? Strozzi	—	Ass.	Ass.	—
34.	AGONY IN GARDEN	A.	A. (g.p.)	? Strozzi	A.	A.	Ass.	Master of *Nativity*
35.	INSTITUTION OF EUCHARIST	A.	A. (g.p.)	? Strozzi	—	Ass.	Ass.	Master of *Nativity*
36.	CHRIST NAILED TO CROSS	A.	A. (g.p.)	A.	—	A.	Ass.	—
37.	CRUCIFIXION	A.	A.	Ass.	—	A.	Ass.	—
38.	CHRIST ON CROSS	—	—	—	Gozzoli	—	—	—
39.	ADORATION OF MAGI	A.	A. (g.p.)	A. (r.)	—	A. (?)	A. (p., r.)	—
42.	CHRIST ON CROSS	A.	—	—	—	A. (p.)	Ass.	—
43.	CHRIST ON CROSS	A.	—	—	—	—	—	—

Abbreviations: A. Fra Angelico Ass. Assistant of Fra Angelico (p.) in part (g.p.) in greater part (r.) restored

from portrait types, like those of Tommaso da Modena preserved in the Sala Capitolare of San Niccolò at Treviso. In the border of the fresco are eleven medallions, that in the centre above containing the pelican with the inscription: SIMILIS FACTVS SVM PELLICANO SOLITVDINIS. The remaining ten medallions show (*left to right*) an unidentified figure with the inscription: DEVS NATVRE PATITVR; Daniel with the inscription: POST EDOMADES VII ET LXII OCCIDET(VR) CHR(ISTV)S; Zacharias with the inscription: HIS PLAGATVS SVM; Jacob with the inscription: AD PRAEDAM DESCENDISTI FILI MI DORMIENS ACCVBVISTI VT LEO; David with the inscription: IN SITI MEA POTAVERVT ME ACETO; Isaiah with the inscription: VERE LANGORES NOSTROS IPSE TVLIT ET DOLORES MEOS; Jeremiah with the inscription: O VOS OMNES QVI TRANSITE PER VIAM ATTENDITE ET VIDETE SI EST DOLOR SICVT DOLOR MEVS; Ezekiel with the inscription: EXALTAVI LIGNVM H(VM)ILE; Job with the inscription: QVIS DET DE CARNIBVS EIVS VT SATVREMVR; and the Erythrean Sibyl with the inscription: MORTE MORIETVR TRIBVS DIEBVS SOMNO SVBSCEPTO TRINO AB INFERIS REGRESSVS AD LVCEM VENIET PRIMVS.

XIX. MASTER OF CELL 2: THE LAMENTATION OVER THE DEAD CHRIST. San Marco, Florence (Cell 2).

XX. MASTER OF CELL 2: THE NATIVITY. San Marco, Florence (Cell 5).

XXI. MASTER OF CELL 2: THE MARIES AT THE SEPULCHRE. San Marco, Florence (Cell 8).

XXII. MASTER OF CELL 2 (?): THE BAPTISM OF CHRIST. San Marco, Florence (Cell 24).

These texts are important for an understanding of the fresco, which shows in the centre the Crucifixion, with the Virgin, the two Maries and St John, and to left and right Saints participating in the mystical sufferings of Christ. On the left are St John Baptist, the patron of Florence, St Mark, the titular saint of the convent, and Saints Lawrence, Cosmas and Damian, the patrons of the Medici. On the right are the founders of religious orders (*kneeling, left to right*) Saints Dominic, Jerome, Francis, Bernard, Giovanni Gualberto and Peter Martyr, and (*standing, left to right*) Saints Ambrose, Augustine, Benedict, Romuald and Thomas Aquinas. Some measure of studio intervention must be presumed in the sometimes flaccid execution of the figures (though not of the heads) of the Saints beneath the Cross, but old photographs (Fig. 12) suggests that many of the figures have been reworked and that their expressiveness has been gravely impaired. The often illustrated head of St Thomas Aquinas is, for example, so heavily retouched as to date in effect from the late nineteenth century. The figure of the good thief is perhaps by Gozzoli. The hand responsible for the half-length prophets in the medallions round the fresco recurs in the *Adoration of the Magi* in Cell 39 (q.v.). The red ground of the fresco is regarded by Douglas (pp. 99–100) and Muratoff (p. 54) as evidence that the fresco was left incomplete. In its present state the red ground is probably due to old restoration, in the course of which the original blue overpainting was removed. The disappearance of this background is (as Marchese, i, p. 255 remarks) accountable for the silhouette-like character of the figures in the frontal plane.

Refectory.

CHRIST ON THE CROSS WITH THE VIRGIN AND SAINT JOHN. A fresco of this subject described in the chronicle of the convent of San Marco (*Annal. Sancti Marci,* f. 6 t.) is assumed by Marchese (i, pp. 257–8) to have been destroyed in 1534 in favour of Sogliani's fresco of *Saint Dominic and his Brethren fed by Angels,* now in the refectory.

Upper Corridor.

CHRIST ON THE CROSS ADORED BY SAINT DOMINIC. Dimensions: 237 × 125 cm. The fresco, situated at the end of the corridor, is a weak variant of the fresco of the same subject in the cloister beneath. Under it is the inscription: SALVE MVNDI SALVTARE. SALVE SALVE IESV CHARE. CRVCI TVAE ME APTARE. VELLEM VERE TV SCIS QVARE. PRESTA MIHI COPIAM. The full text of this hymn appears in Migne (*Patr. Lat.,* clxxxiv, 1319).

THE ANNUNCIATION. (Plates 98, 101, 102.) Dimensions: 216 × 321 cm. Situated on the inner wall of the corridor facing the staircase. Beneath the fresco is the painted inscription: VIRGINIS INTACTE CVM VENERIS ANTE FIGVRAM PRE-TEREVNDO CAVE NE SILEATVR AVE. Above this is an incised inscription of uncertain date: SALVE MATER PIETATIS ET TOTIVS TRINITATIS NOBILE TRICLINIVM. In composition the fresco is more closely related to the *Annunciation* at Madrid than to the other *Annunciation* altarpieces, and perhaps formed the source of this painting. The design (one of the richest and most satisfying in Angelico's work) and the greater part of the execution are by the master, and the discrepancies between this fresco and the fresco of the same subject in Cell 3 are a matter of date and not of quality (see below). The two types of capital shown in the loggia derive from capitals employed by Michelozzo in the cloisters of the Annunziata and of San Marco.

THE VIRGIN AND CHILD ENTHRONED WITH EIGHT SAINTS. (Plates 97, 99, 100.) Dimensions: 205 × 276 cm. The fresco, situated on the inner wall of the east corridor, shows (*left*) Saints Dominic, Cosmas, Damian and Mark, and (*right*) John the Evangelist, Thomas Aquinas, Lawrence and Peter Martyr. The composition is consistent with a somewhat later dating than the Bosco ai Frati altarpiece, and the fresco (along with the *Annunciation*) was perhaps executed after Angelico's return from Rome. The extent of studio intervention has been exaggerated. The two outer saints are inferior in quality to the six inner figures, and are perhaps by the Master of Cell 2 (see below).

Cells.

1. NOLI ME TANGERE. (Plates 84, 85.) Dimensions: 177 × 139 cm. Assigned to an assistant of Angelico by Van Marle (x, p. 77) and Muratoff (p. 57), and by Bazin to the so-called Master of the *Annunciation.* There is no reason to doubt that the cartoon of this fresco is by Angelico, and that the two figures are wholly by his hand. Noteworthy is the practice of silhouetting the two heads, one against a rock, the other against a wooden fence, and the colour, which has the luminosity typical of the autograph frescoes.

2. THE LAMENTATION. (Figure XIX.) Dimensions: 104 × 162 cm. The group of four kneeling figures surrounding the dead Christ was perhaps adapted in reverse from the corresponding group in the Croce al Tempio *Lamentation* in the Museo di San Marco. Neither the cartoon of the fresco nor its execution is by Angelico. The artist responsible for painting it is characterized by thin types with pointed noses and furrows between the eyes, flat forms and constricted drapery. Throughout the present book this hand is denominated the Master of Cell 2.

3. THE ANNUNCIATION. (Plates 83, 86.) Dimensions: 187 × 157 cm. Wholly by Angelico save for the small figure of St Peter Martyr on the left which is an interpolation by the Master of Cell 2.

4. CHRIST ON THE CROSS WITH SAINT JOHN THE EVANGELIST, THE VIRGIN, AND SAINTS DOMINIC AND JEROME. Dimensions: 189 × 157 cm. Design and execution are by the Master of Cell 2. The Christ on the Cross depends from the corresponding figure in the fresco in the cloister beneath.

5. THE NATIVITY. (Figure XX.) Dimensions: 189 × 150 cm. Executed by the Master of Cell 2. The design is, however, more coherent than that of the frescoes in Cells 2 and 4, and it is possible that the figures of the Virgin, St Joseph and the Child, and the rectangular stable depend from a drawing by Angelico.

6. THE TRANSFIGURATION. (Plates 93–96.) Dimensions: 189 × 159 cm. This splendid scheme was designed and executed by Angelico. Marchese (1853, p. 39) reports the foreground figures as much damaged.

7. THE MOCKING OF CHRIST. (Plates 87, 88.) Dimensions: 195 × 159 cm. The composition, and the execution of the figure of Christ and of the head to His left, are due to Angelico. The seated figures of the Virgin and of St Dominic in the foreground were perhaps executed by the Master of Cell 2 after the master's cartoon. There is a strip of repaint round three sides of the fresco, and a large made-up area above; the fresco may originally have been rectangular.

XXIII. MASTER OF CELL 2 (?): CHRIST CARRYING
THE CROSS. San Marco, Florence (Cell 28).

XXIV. MASTER OF CELL 31: CHRIST IN LIMBO.
San Marco, Florence (Cell 31).

XXV. MASTER OF CELL 31: THE SERMON ON
THE MOUNT. San Marco, Florence (Cell 32).

XXVI. MASTER OF CELL 36: CHRIST NAILED TO
THE CROSS. San Marco, Florence (Cell 36).

8. THE MARIES AT THE SEPULCHRE. (Figure XXI.) Dimensions: 182 × 155 cm. Designed and executed by the Master of Cell 2. The figure of the angel and of the Virgin peering down into the tomb probably depend from drawings by Angelico, who may also have been responsible for the execution of the angel's head. The Christ is restored. There is much local retouching in the background and elsewhere.

9. THE CORONATION OF THE VIRGIN. (Plates 91, 92.) Dimensions: 189 × 159 cm. Designed and executed by Angelico. Below are the kneeling figures of (*left to right*) Saints Thomas Aquinas, Benedict, Dominic, Francis, Peter Martyr and (?) Mark. A variant of the two main figures is found on one of two circular panels with *Christ on the Cross between the Virgin and Saint John Evangelist* and *The Coronation of the Virgin* (diameter: 19 cm.) in the Museo di San Marco, painted by an imitator of Angelico, perhaps the Master of Cell 2. These panels were at one time in the Cappella di San Luca in the Ss. Annunziata, and seem originally to have come from Santa Maria della Croce al Tempio (Paatz, i, pp. 135, 196).

10. THE PRESENTATION IN THE TEMPLE. (Plates 89, 90.) Dimensions: 151 × 131 cm. The central figures seem to have been executed by Angelico. The subsidiary figures of St Peter Martyr and the Beata Villana were repainted before the middle of the nineteenth century (Marchese, 1853, p. 36). The fresco was originally rectangular.

11. THE VIRGIN AND CHILD ENTHRONED WITH SAINTS ZENOBIUS AND THOMAS AQUINAS. Dimensions: 189 × 159 cm. Designed and executed by the Master of Cell 2. The spatial scheme depends from that of *The Mocking of Christ*. Old photographs show that this fresco was extensively damaged and has been heavily retouched. The fresco was perhaps originally rectangular.

15–22. These eight cells contain frescoes of *Christ on the Cross*, which appear to be the work of a single hand, perhaps that responsible for the execution of the *Christ on the Cross adored by Saint Dominic* in the corridor. The level of execution is below that of the frescoes associable with the Master of Cell 2, and in no case can the compositions be ascribed to Angelico.

23. CHRIST ON THE CROSS WITH THE VIRGIN AND SAINT PETER MARTYR. Designed and executed by the Master of Cell 2.

24. THE BAPTISM OF CHRIST. (Figure XXII.) Dimensions: 187 × 156 cm. The scene differs in style from the preceding frescoes, but probably represents a later phase in the evolution of the Master of Cell 2. This and the following frescoes are less closely related to Angelico than the frescoes on the opposite side of the corridor.

25. CHRIST ON THE CROSS WITH THE VIRGIN, SAINT MARY MAGDALEN AND SAINT DOMINIC. Dimensions: 189 × 145 cm. This scene is by the same hand as the preceding fresco.

26. CHRIST AS MAN OF SORROWS WITH THE VIRGIN AND SAINT THOMAS AQUINAS. By the same hand as the fresco in Cell 24. The blindfold head of Christ in the upper right corner of the fresco and the seated Virgin in the left foreground are loosely dependent on *The Mocking of Christ* in Cell 7.

27. CHRIST AT THE COLUMN WITH THE VIRGIN AND SAINT DOMINIC. Probably by the same hand as the fresco in Cell 24.

28. CHRIST CARRYING THE CROSS WITH THE VIRGIN AND SAINT DOMINIC. (Figure XXIII.) Dimensions: 158 × 140 cm. Probably by the same hand as the fresco in Cell 24.

31. CHRIST IN LIMBO. (Figure XXIV.) Dimensions: 195 × 177 cm. The fresco is by a new hand, which was responsible for decorating the following five cells. In each case the composition is more elaborate than those of the preceding frescoes, with a tendency towards circular construction and a cursive handling of the drapery which are reminiscent of miniature illumination. None of the scenes was designed by Angelico. The artist responsible for these frescoes is tentatively identified by D'Ancona (pp. 92–4) and Van Marle (x, pp. 88–9) with the miniaturist Zanobi Strozzi, and with the artist responsible for the concluding panels of the Annunziata silver chest (see pp. 190–3). In the few cases where direct comparison is possible, and particularly in the two scenes of *Christ in Limbo*, the version on panel is more closely related to Angelico than the version in fresco, and in no case can the two works be by a single hand. In the present volume the author of the frescoes is denominated the Master of Cell 31. The identification of this artist with Zanobi Strozzi is doubtful.

32. THE SERMON ON THE MOUNT. (Figure XXV.) Dimensions: 193 × 200 cm. Designed and executed by the Master of Cell 31.

33. THE ARREST OF CHRIST. Dimensions: 189 × 188 cm. Designed and executed by the Master of Cell 31.

33A. THE TEMPTATION OF CHRIST. Fragmentary fresco, in part destroyed by the construction of a window in the north corridor. Designed and executed by the Master of Cell 31. A fresco of *Christ's Entry into Jerusalem* in the adjacent cell (33B) has been largely destroyed (Marchese, 1853, p. 38).

34. THE AGONY IN THE GARDEN. Dimensions: 189 × 157 cm. Designed and executed by the Master of Cell 31. As noted by Beissel (p. 36) the watching figures of the Virgin and Martha (an unusual feature in the iconography of this scene) are contrasted with the sleeping apostles opposite. The figures of the two women are given by Salmi (1950, p. 154) to Gozzoli.

35. THE INSTITUTION OF THE EUCHARIST. Dimensions: 196 × 244 cm. Designed and executed by the Master of Cell 31. The illusionistic treatment of the windows, with their fictive view across the cloister of the convent, is a notable feature of the composition. This rare scene is also included in the cycle of panels on the silver chest, where it replaces the more usual *Last Supper*, and is accompanied by the words (*John*, vi, 54): QVI MANDVCAT MEAM CARNEM ET BIBIT MEVM SANGVINEM HABET VITAM AETERNAM. An altarpiece of the same subject, painted by Justus of Ghent in 1473 for the Compagnia di Corpus Domini at Urbino, is in the Galleria Nazionale delle Marche at Urbino.

36. CHRIST NAILED TO THE CROSS. (Figure XXVI.) Dimensions: 181 × 144 cm. Designed and executed by an assistant. The hand responsible for this fresco is more closely connected with Angelico than the Master of Cell 31, and stands in the same relation to the master as the Master of Cell 2, from whom he is distinguished by thick-set figures and heavier forms.

This artist, denominated in this volume the Master of Cell 36, is identical with one of the assistants employed by Angelico on the frescoes in the Vatican. Salmi (1950, p. 154) detects the intervention of Gozzoli. From the mouth of Christ run the words: PR DIMICTE ILLIS QVIA NES(CIVNT QVID FACIVNT). Beissel (p. 40) refers the unusual iconography of this scene to a passage in the *Vitae Christi* of St Bonaventure (c. 78, in *Opera S. Bonventurae*, Lugdini, vi, 1668, p. 388), from which details of the representation (including the three ladders supporting Christ and the executioners) are drawn.

37. THE CRUCIFIXION WITH SAINT JOHN THE EVANGELIST, THE VIRGIN, AND SAINTS DOMINIC AND (?) THOMAS AQUINAS. Dimensions: 290 × 179 cm. Designed and executed by the Master of Cell 36. The representation of the bad thief depends from that in the *Crucifixion* in the Sala del Capitolo.

38. CHRIST ON THE CROSS WITH THE VIRGIN AND SAINTS JOHN THE EVANGELIST, COSMAS AND PETER MARTYR. Like the frescoes in Cells 40, 41 and 44, this scene, with the *Pietà* beneath, has escaped a direct ascription to Angelico. It is regarded by Venturi (pp. 70–2) as an early work of Gozzoli. The hand recurs in the damaged *Adoration of the Magi* in Cell 39.

39. THE ADORATION OF THE MAGI. (Plate 77.) Dimensions: 180 × 360 cm. Probably designed by Angelico. The fresco was restored in the middle of the nineteenth century by Professor Antonio Marini, and no verdict is now possible as to the part played by the master in its execution. The forms on the left side in particular have been materially changed. In style it is most closely connected with the *Crucifixion* in the Sala del Capitolo, and at least on the right reveals the intervention of Benozzo Gozzoli. The fresco has been assigned to the years 1439 (on account of the presence of oriental costumes, presumed to have been inspired by the Council held in Florence in this year), 1441 (for no evident reason) and 1442–43 (in preparation for or in commemoration of the occupation of the cell by Pope Eugenius IV at the time of the consecration of San Marco). The cell was occupied by Cosimo de' Medici (for whom it was constructed). Paatz (iii, p. 74) relates the subject to the Compagnia dei tre Magi, which was directed from San Marco and with which the Medici were associated.

40, 41, 44. CHRIST ON THE CROSS. These works are of low quality, and have never received a direct ascription to Angelico.

42. CHRIST ON THE CROSS WITH (?) SAINT MARK, LONGINUS, SAINT DOMINIC, THE VIRGIN AND SAINT MARY MAGDALEN. Dimensions: 208 × 205 cm. Designed and executed by the Master of Cell 36.

43. CHRIST ON THE CROSS WITH THE VIRGIN AND SAINTS JOHN THE EVANGELIST, MARY MAGDALEN AND DOMINIC. Designed and executed by the Master of Cell 36. The fresco was originally painted on an external wall of the corridor, and later enclosed in a cell.

In so far as condition is concerned, it must be noted that in a number of cases the shape or size of the cell frescoes has been modified. Thus in *The Mocking of Christ* in Cell 7 there are additions to right and left and the upper part of the fresco (which must originally have been rectangular) has been made up. The fictive frames of the frescoes seem in practically every case to be of comparatively recent date. In the aggregate these frames and the addition of areas of modern paint serve to weaken the impact of the frescoes.

There is no firm evidence for the date at which the frescoes were begun. The Dominican community took possession of the premises of San Marco Nuovo in 1436, and the rebuilding of the church and convent was initiated by Michelozzo (on the commission of Cosimo and Lorenzo de' Medici, who had been instrumental in securing the premises for the Dominicans) in 1437. The *cappella maggiore* of the church was completed in 1439, and the church was dedicated at Epiphany 1443. All sources agree that in 1437 the convent buildings were in ruinous condition. According to the chronicle of Fra Giuliano Lappacini, cited by Marchese (i, p. 77), forty-four cells were completed by 1443. It is unlikely that the cell frescoes on the upper floor were begun before this year. A *terminus ante quem* for the completion of those executed by Angelico is provided by the artist's departure for Rome in 1446–7. The cloister frescoes and the *Crucifixion* in the Sala del Capitolo may have been painted at any time after 1438.

Bearing in mind these dates and the analysis of the frescoes given above, it may be inferred that the frescoes on the ground floor, which are wholly by Angelico and members of his studio, precede those on the floor above. In style and handling the *Crucifixion* in the Sala del Capitolo is closely linked with the *Adoration of the Magi* in Cell 39, and it is likely that the latter was the first fresco completed on the upper floor. Both of these scenes were probably painted on the commission of Cosimo de' Medici. The scenes on the upper floor for which Angelico was directly responsible are limited to six cells on the outer side of one corridor and to two frescoes on the corridor walls. There is a marked discrepancy of style between these two groups of scenes, and it is very probable that the second of them (comprising the *Annunciation* and the *Virgin and Child with eight Saints*) was painted after Angelico's return from Rome in 1449. Of the frescoes in the cells the foreground figures in *The Transfiguration* most clearly anticipate the style of the upper cycle of frescoes in the Vatican. In work in these and the contiguous cells (1–11) Angelico was assisted by an artist, the Master of Cell 2, whose hand appears for the first time in the predella of the Cortona polyptych. The hand of this painter is sometimes evident in frescoes substantially executed by Angelico, and is sometimes found in isolation. Though strongly influenced by Angelico, his role was not limited to reproducing the master's cartoons, and certain of his frescoes must be regarded as independent inventions within the framework of Angelico's style. There is no trace of the hand of this artist in the frescoes in the Vatican, and this lends support to the view that he may also have executed the frescoes in Cells 24–28 after 1447 when Angelico left Florence. The indebtedness of these scenes to Angelico is considerably less marked than in the frescoes in Cells 2, 4, 5, 8, 11 and 23. Four frescoes in cells to the right of the staircase (36, 37, 42 and 43) again reflect Angelico's style. Like the Master of Cell 2, the Master of Cell 36 must have been a member of Angelico's studio, and seems to have worked under the general guidance, but without the active intervention, of the master. It is possible that this master was responsible for painting (from Angelico's cartoon) the drapery of certain figures in the *Crucifixion* in the Sala del Capitolo, and served as an assistant of Angelico in the *Scenes from the Life of Saint Stephen* in the Vatican. The third hand apparent in the frescoes in the cells, the Master of Cell 31, is less intimately related to Angelico. The frescoes in Cells 15–22, 40, 41 and 44 are of low quality; the hand or hands responsible for these frescoes presumably served in a subordinate capacity in Angelico's studio.

SCENES FROM THE LIVES OF SAINTS STEPHEN AND LAWRENCE. Chapel of Nicholas V, Vatican.

PLATES 103–120. FIGS. 13, XXVII, XXVIII.

There is no evidence of Angelico's presence in Rome before March 1447, when he was engaged in painting 'la chapella di santo Pietro'. It is, however, generally assumed that he had been summoned to Rome at least some months earlier. Pacchioni ('Gli ultimi anni del Beato Angelico', in *L'Arte*, xii, 1909, pp. 2–3), working from statements of Razzi (*Vite dei Santi e Beati Toscani*, i, 1593, p. 746) and Castiglioni (in *Acta Sanctorum*, ad loc.) that Angelico's arrival in Rome preceded the appointment of Sant'Antonino as Archbishop of Florence in March 1445, supposes that Angelico reached Rome in January or February of this year. Since Angelico was certainly at work in Rome seven days after the election of Nicholas V as Pope (6 March 1447), the statement of Vasari (ii, p. 516) that 'papa Niccola V mandò per lui' can hardly be correct, and his employment in the Vatican must be ascribed to the intervention of Eugenius IV (d. 13 February 1447).

The documentary references to Angelico's activity in Rome relate to two separate commissions, the first the painting of 'la chapella di santo Pietro' and the second to 'dipinture de lo studio di N.S.' In addition there survives a cycle of frescoes by Angelico in the Chapel of Nicholas V in the Vatican, and a description by Vasari of a further fresco cycle of *Scenes from the Life of Christ* in the demolished Chapel of St Nicholas (Cappella del SS. Sacramento) (see p. 207). The entry referring to the painting of the studio of Nicholas V is transcribed by Müntz (*Les Arts à la Cour des Papes*, i, 1878, p. 112): '1449. A spese fatte questo anno nela fabrica di palazzo . . . da di primo di Genaro . . . di 31 di Dicembre . . . d'ogni sorta duc. 182, bol. 62, den. 8 in dipinture de lo studio di N.S. cioe per salario di Fra Giovanni di Fi (renze) e suoi gharzoni, e altre chosette. . . .' A later payment of 16 March 1451 to the glass painter Fra Giovanni da Roma 'per due finestre di vetro biancho a fatte nelo studio di N.S., una con santo Lorenzo e santo Stefano, e nel altra la nostra donna' (Müntz, op. cit., p. 128) was regarded by Müntz as proof that the 'studio di N.S.' was identical with the Chapel of Nicholas V. This inference is accepted by most students of Fra Angelico. Biagetti, however, ('Una nuova ipotesi intorno allo studio e alla cappella di Niccolo V nel Palazzo Vaticano', in *Atti della Pontificia Accademia Romana di Archeologia*, iv, 1933, pp. 205–14) proves conclusively that the payment of 1451 to Fra Giovanni da Roma cannot, on account of the dimensions of the windows, refer, as Müntz assumed, to the windows of the Chapel of Nicholas V, and that the design of the pavement of the supposed studio, for which payment was made to Verrone di Agnolo da Firenze in 1451, from the first presupposed the presence of an altar. There were thus two separate commissions, one for the Chapel of Nicholas V, which is referred to throughout the documents as the 'cappella segreta del papa', 'cappelletta piccola della sala prima', and 'cappelletta piccola di palazzo', and the other for the studio, which would have been near or adjacent to the Chapel and was presumably destroyed when this part of the Vatican was restored by Pope Julius II. The studio is probably identical with the 'stanza di lavoro', of which an inventory was made after the death of Nicholas V in 1455. Work in the studio was under way in 1449. Papini ('Riguardo al soggiorno dell'

Angelico in Roma', in *L'Arte*, xiii, 1910, pp. 138–9) infers from the recorded payments that Angelico worked in the studio for little more than half of this year, and that the frescoed decoration was in all probability completed when Gozzoli, Angelico's principal assistant in Rome, arrived at Orvieto in July 1449. The frescoes were certainly completed before March 1450, when provision was made for the gilding of the frieze.

The frescoes in the Chapel of Nicholas V have been assigned alternatively to the brackets 1447–9 and 1453–5. Schottmüller (p. 236) and Wingenroth (pp. 114 f.) believe the frescoes to have been executed in part before 1449 and in part after 1453. Van Marle (x, pp. 120–1) and Muratoff (p. 66) refer the entire decoration of the chapel to the later date. A document of 15 February 1448, recording a payment 'pro duabus libris azuri ultramarini pro pictura capelae secretae D.N. Papae' (Müntz, op. cit., ii, p. 316), though it makes no mention of Fra Angelico, certainly refers to the decoration of the Chapel; and it is assumed by Biagetti that this was begun early in 1448 and was completed before 1451, when the pavement of the Chapel was renewed. Van Marle (x, p. 121) wrongly refers the date A.D. CCLIII on the *Saint Lawrence before Decius* to the year 1453.

This speculation is superfluous, in that three documents published by Müntz (op. cit., i, 1878, pp. 126–7) offer a precise date for the execution of the frescoes. These documents read as follows:

1447. 9 May. A Pietro Jachoo da Furli dipintore a lavorato chon frate Giovanni a la chapella di santo Pietro adi detto fl. 3, b. 15, e quali ebbe di suo salario di qo. mexe e XVIII di e stato a lavorare, cioe s'e partito dadi XIII di Marzo perinfino adi die di Maggio e fo al bast. I a fo. 809 (?) . . . a sua rag.–T.S. 1447, fol. 37.

1447. 23 May. A frate Giovanni di Pietro dipintore a la chapella di sto. Pietro dell'ordine di san Domenicho adi XXIII di Maggio d. quaranta tre, b. vinti sette, sono per la provisione di d. 200 l'anno dadi 13 di Marzo perinfino adi ultimo di Maggio prossimo a venire: f. XLIII, b. XXVII. – A Benozo da Leso dipintore da Firenze a la sopradetta chapella adi detto f. diciotto, b. dodici, e quali sono per sua provisione di f. VII il mexe dadi XIII di Marzo sino adi ultimo di Maggio prossimo: fl. XVIII, b. XII. – A Giovanni d'Antonio della Checha dipintore a la detta chapella adi detto d. due, b. quaranta due, sono per la provisione di mexi 2 2/5 a f. uno il mexe e finira (?) a di ultimo di Maggio prossimo: fl. II, b. XLII. – A Jachomo d'Antonio da Poli dipintore ala detta chapella adi XXIII di Maggio fl. tre, sono per la sua provisione di 3 mexe e quali debano finire a di ultimo di Maggio prossimo a f. I il mexe: f. III, b. O. – T.S. 1447, ff. 38 v. et 39.

1447. 1 June. A frate Giovanni da Firenze che dipigne nela chapella di sº Pietro adi detto f. due, b. trenta nove, sono per choxe assgº avere spexi per bisogni di detta chapella: fl. II, b. XXXVIIII.–Ibid., 1.39 v.

It is assumed by Beissel (p. 89) and other writers on Fra Angelico that the 'chapella di santo Pietro' to which these documents refer is identical with the Cappella del Sacramento or Cappella di San Niccolò, which contained the *Scenes from the Life of Christ* by Fra Angelico described by Vasari (q.v.). An analysis by Egger ('Capella Sancti Nicolai (Cappella del SS. Sacramento)' in Ehrle and Egger, *Der Vatikanische Palast in seiner Entwicklung bis zur Mitte des XV. Jahrhunderts*, 1935, p. 133) leaves no doubt that this identification is incorrect. The sense of the documents is elucidated by a passage in the record of a meeting held at Orvieto on 11 May of the same year (quoted in full on p. 189), in which it is stated that 'ad presens in Urbe sit quidam frater observantie sancti Dominici, qui pinsit et pingit *cappellam Smi. D.N. in*

XXVII. FRA ANGELICO: SAINT JEROME.
Chapel of Nicholas V. Vatican.

XXVIII. FRA ANGELICO: SAINT THOMAS AQUINAS.
Chapel of Nicholas V, Vatican.

palatio apostolico sancti Petri de Urbe.' In view of the coincidence of date, this passage cannot apply to any other work than that to which the payments of 9 and 23 May 1447 relate. Equally the term 'cappellam Smi. D.N.' can refer only to the secret chapel of the Pope, that is the Chapel of Nicholas V, and we must therefore conclude that the payments noted by Müntz are connected with work not in the basilica of St Peter's but in the Vatican Palace (the words 'chapella di sto. Pietro' being a contraction of the more detailed description given in the Orvieto document), and that this work was the painting of the private chapel of the Pope. Having regard to the number of assistants employed by Angelico in Rome and to the fact that the two completed sections of the ceiling of the Cappella di San Brizio at Orvieto were executed in less than four months, we may suppose that work in the studio and the chapel of Nicholas V was concluded by the summer of 1449.

The Chapel of Nicholas V is described by Vasari (loc. cit.): 'Per quanti tanti lavori essendo chiara per tutta Italia la fama di Fra Giovanni, papa Niccola V mandò per lui, ed in Roma gli fece fare la cappella del palazzo, dove il papa ode la messa, con un Deposto di Croce ed alcune storie di San Lorenzo, bellissime.' The *Deposition*, which presumably served as an altarpiece, has disappeared. The narrative frescoes are arranged in two tiers, and comprise six *Scenes from the Life of Saint Stephen* (above) and five *Scenes from the Life of Saint Lawrence* (below). These show: (i) on the wall to the right of the entrance (above) *The Ordination of Saint Stephen* and *Saint Stephen distributing Alms*, (below) *The Ordination of Saint Lawrence*; (ii) on the entrance wall (above) *Saint Stephen preaching* and *Saint Stephen addressing the Council*, (below) *Saint Lawrence receiving the Treasures of the Church from Pope Sixtus II* and *Saint Lawrence distributing Alms*; and (iii) on the wall to the left of the entrance (above) *The Expulsion of Saint*

Stephen and *The Stoning of Saint Stephen*, (below) *Saint Lawrence before Decius* and *The Martyrdom of Saint Lawrence*. Flanking the frescoes on the lateral walls are eight full-length Saints (below) Saints Jerome (transformed into a figure of St Bonaventure) (Fig. XXVII), Thomas Aquinas (Fig. XXVIII), Athanasius and John Chrysostom, (above) Saints Augustine, Ambrose, Leo and Gregory the Great. On the roof of the chapel are the four Evangelists. Below the lower frescoes are traces of a polychrome textile pattern which originally completed the scheme (for this see *Ecclesia*, 1951).

The entire fresco cycle is extensively restored. Inscriptions in the chapel record restorations in the last quarter of the sixteenth century by Pope Gregory XIII, in 1712 by Pope Clement XI, and in 1815 by Pope Pius VII. An account of local restoration of the frescoes on the roof and walls, made necessary by lesions in the ground, as a result of which traces were revealed of the naturalistic blue sky in the lateral frescoes and of the painted drapery with the stemma of Nicholas V on the lower part of the wall, is given by Biagetti (in *Atti della Pontificia Accademia Romana*, serie iii, *Rendiconti*, iii, 1925, pp. 485–92). General restoration of the frescoes was undertaken in 1947–51, and the reproductions in the present volume show them in their cleaned state. The narrative frescoes fall into two classes, those which are seriously abraded (of which *The Martyrdom of Saint Lawrence* on the left wall is the most seriously damaged), and those which have been much repainted and restored (*The Preaching of Saint Stephen* and *Saint Lawrence receiving the Treasures of the Church* are salient examples of this). Of the full-length figures the *Saint Athanasius* and *Saint John Chrysostom* have been transferred to canvas and are gravely damaged. A clear account of the results of the cleaning of 1947–51 is given by De Campos (in *Atti della Pontificia Accademia Romana di Archeologia*, xxiii–iv, 1950, pp. 385–8).

It is established that in 1447 Angelico's studio comprised Benozzo Gozzoli, who received a relatively high remuneration, Giovanni di Antonio della Cecha (probably identical with a Giovanni di Antonio da Firenze, who later in the year was killed on the scaffolding at Orvieto), Carlo di ser Lazaro da Narni and Giacomo d'Antonio da Poli. All of these artists may have been employed in the Chapel of Nicholas V. The part played by Gozzoli in the execution of the frescoes has been analysed by Pacchioni ('Gli inizi artistici di Benozzo Gozzoli', in *L'Arte*, xiii, 1910, pp. 423–42) and Wingenroth (*Die Jugendwerke des Benozzo Gozzoli*, 1897, pp. 69–80). In the narrative scenes the execution of the figures may be tentatively distributed as follows:

The Ordination of Saint Stephen. The two foremost figures and the third apostle from the left by Angelico; the first, second, fifth and (?) sixth apostles from the left by Gozzoli.

Saint Stephen distributing Alms. The Saint, the acolyte in the left background and the woman in the centre by Angelico; two women on the right and the male figure advancing with a hat by Gozzoli.

Saint Stephen preaching. The much damaged Saint and at least four seated women in the foreground by Angelico; woman in full-face, other women in middle ground and two standing men on right of background by Gozzoli.

Saint Stephen addressing the Council. Largely by Angelico; heads in background on right and (?) two standing figures on left by Gozzoli.

The Expulsion of Saint Stephen. The Saint and the bearded man holding a stone by Angelico; two men on extreme left and male figure in centre by Gozzoli.

The Stoning of Saint Stephen. Largely by Angelico; three male heads on left and (?) man in centre by Gozzoli.

The Ordination of Saint Lawrence. Largely by Angelico; three acolytes and deacon on right by Gozzoli.

Saint Lawrence receiving the Treasures of the Church. Saint and attendant behind largely repainted. Pope by Angelico; head in background and (?) figures on left by Gozzoli.

Saint Lawrence distributing Alms. Saint by Angelico. Woman with child on left, woman in left centre and male heads on right by Gozzoli.

Saint Lawrence before Decius. Probably largely by Angelico. Soldier in helmet, male figure behind Saint and five heads on extreme right by Gozzoli.

The Martyrdom of Saint Lawrence. Figures in window, Saint and executioner on left by Angelico; figures above and (?) much damaged executioners on right by Gozzoli.

The hands of at least two other assistants are apparent in the frescoes. Muratoff (pp. 68–70) denies Angelico's responsibility for the cartoons of the St Stephen frescoes, and greatly restricts the scale of his intervention in the lower scenes. There can, however, be little doubt that Angelico was responsible for all of the cartoons of the narrative frescoes. Van Marle (x, pp. 122–32) correctly notes that the part executed by Angelico is greater in the lower (and more visible) than in the upper (and less visible) scenes. Examination suggests that each of the frescoes was, in a loose sense, collaborative, and that two or more artists worked on each field. Van Marle's attempt to attribute the whole of the second, fifth and sixth scenes of the legend of St Stephen to an unnamed assistant of Angelico is inadmissible.

Two sheets of drawings contain what have sometimes been claimed as preliminary studies for the Vatican frescoes. These are:

(i) Cambridge, Fitzwilliam Museum.
Recto: Saint Matthew. Bistre heightened in white on a greenish prepared ground.
Verso: Saint Luke. Bistre and wash on white paper.
Dimensions: 16×15 cm.
The *recto* is related by Hind (in *Vasari Society*, II, v, Ia and Ib) to the St Matthew in the Chapel of Nicholas V. Berenson (*The Drawings of the Florentine Painters*, 1938, iii, p. 16, No. 161A) accepts the St Luke as by Angelico and the St Matthew as by Gozzoli.

(ii) Windsor Castle, Royal Library (12812).
Recto: Head of a Saint. Sepia and white on buff prepared paper.
Verso: Studies of Saint Lawrence, a Woman carrying a Child and a standing male Figure.
Dimensions: 18×16 cm.
The studies on the *verso* correspond with the figures of St Lawrence and the woman carrying a child in the fresco of *Saint Lawrence distributing Alms*, and that of the male figure with a standing man second from right in the fresco of *Saint Lawrence before Decius*. Berenson (op. cit., ii, p. 17, No. 163, and i, pp. 4–5) accepts both drawings as by Angelico, and regards the *verso* as a preliminary study for the corresponding parts of the two frescoes. Popham (*The Italian Drawings of the XV and XVI Centuries in the Collection of His Majesty the King at Windsor Castle*, 1949, p. 172, No. 10) follows Papini ('Dai disegni di Benozzo Gozzoli', in *L'Arte*, xiii, 1910, p. 290) in giving both *recto* and *verso* to Gozzoli. The *verso* seems to depend from the related figures in the frescoes, but Angelico's authorship of the *recto* cannot be ruled out. Venturi (p. 81 n.) tentatively connects the *recto* with the lost frescoes in the Cappella del Sacramento.

CHRIST IN GLORY: PROPHETS. Duomo, Orvieto.
PLATES 121, 122.

The documents which enable us to trace the story of Angelico's frescoes at Orvieto have been published by Luzzi (*Il Duomo d'Orvieto descritto ed illustrato*, 1866, p. 433) and Fumi (*Il Duomo di Orvieto*, 1891, pp. 393–5) and are reprinted by Douglas (pp. 184–7). They comprise:

(i) A letter from a Benedictine monk, Don Francesco di Barone da Perugia, to the Camarlingo of the Fabbrica of the Duomo at Orvieto notifying the latter that Angelico, who was then in Rome, had expressed his willingness to come to Orvieto for the following summer (1447).

(ii) The record of a meeting at Orvieto on 11 May of the same year, in which the *operai* of the Duomo take note of the fact that the Chapel of the Corporal (or the Cappella della Madonna di San Brizio) in the south transept of the cathedral has not yet been painted, 'et pro honore dicte Ecclesie est dipingenda per aliquem bonum et famosum magistrum pictorem, et ad presens in Urbe sit quidam frater observantie sancti Dominici, qui pinsit et pingit cappellam Smi. D.N. in palatio apostolico sancti Petri de Urbe, qui forte veniret ad pingendam dictam cappellam, et est famosus ultra omnes alios pictores ytalicos et staret ad pingendum in dicta cappella tantum tribus in anno mensibus, vid: junio, julio et augusto, quia aliis mensibus opportet eum servire Smo. D.N. et in dictis tribus mensibus non vult stare Rome, et petit salarium pro se ad rationem ducentorum ducatorum auri in anno et cum expensis ciborum, et quod sibi dentur colores expensis Fabrice, et fiant pontes expensis Fabrice, item vult pro uno suo consortio ducatos septem auri de auro et pro duobus aliis famulis tres ducatos auri, vid: in mense pro quolibet ipsorum et cum expensis ipsorum; habitis inter eos pluribus collocutionibus, delib: quod dictus Enrigus miles possit conducere pro dicta Fabrica et etiam dictus Camerarius dictum magistrum pictorem cum dictis consortio et famulo cum dictis salariis et expensis et aliis petitis, dummodo promictat servire laborerium totius picture dicte cappelle vel saltem servire in dicta pictura dictis tribus mensibus quolibet anno quousque finiverit totum laborerium. Et vocatur dictus magister pictor frater Johannes.' (Orvieto, Archivio dell'Opera del Duomo. Rif. 1443–8, c. 284 t.)

(iii) A payment of 26 August 1447 to 'Giovanni compagno overo garzone di m. frate Giovanni dipentore' covering the expenses of journeys to Florence to buy ultramarine and to Rome to purchase other colours. (Orvieto, Archivio dell'Opera del Duomo. Cam. 1445–50.)

(iv) An entry of 28 September 1447, noting that the sum due to Angelico for three months' work at Orvieto had been paid. (Orvieto, Archivio dell'Opera del Duomo. Rif. 1443–8, c. 287 t.)

(v) A more detailed document of the same date, in which Angelico (on his own behalf and on that of his three assistants 'Benozzo Lesi de Florentia, Johannis Antonii de Florentia, et Jacobus de Poli') acknowledges the settlement of the sum due. (Orvieto, Archivio dell'Opera del Duomo. Rif. 1443–8, c. 298.)

(vi) A final payment of 30 September 1447 'ad frate m. Giovanni pentore per la provisione sua et di compagni, cioe per tre mesi et mezo che anno servito ad depegnere nella capella nuova – ducati d'ore cento tre e mezo. Item ad Benozzo per le spese che fecero nell' albergo prima che essi fusseri conducti.' (Orvieto, Archivio dell'Opera del Duomo. Cam. 1445–50.)

Angelico did not return to Orvieto after 1447, and the contract for the frescoes was broken in 1449. Document (ii) appears to provide for the complete painting of the chapel (later undertaken by Signorelli). As was usual, work began on the roof, where two of the four triangular spaces were finished when Angelico left Orvieto. These show a *Christ in Majesty with Angels* and *Sixteen Prophets*; below the latter are the words PROPHETARVM LAVDABILIS NVMERVS. Muratoff (p. 65) assumes that the execution of the frescoes was entrusted entirely to assistants. This can hardly have been the case, and, as noted by Van Marle (x, pp. 106–7), a number of the heads in the upper part of the second fresco were probably painted by Angelico. Schottmüller (p. 265) and Douglas (p. 140) rightly deny that the figure of Christ in the first fresco is due to an assistant; owing to damage to the ground, this figure is extensively restored. Pacchioni ('Gli inizi artistici di Benozzo Gozzoli', in *L'Arte*, xiii, 1910, p. 426) ascribes the angels to the right of Christ in *Christ in Majesty* to Gozzoli, and three of those to the left (which are much damaged) to Angelico. In the second fresco three of the prophets (the first and third in the central row reading from the top and a figure to their right) are related in type to Gozzoli, who was also perhaps responsible for the drapery of the foreground figures and for many of the heads in the borders of the two frescoes. Salmi (1950, pp. 155–6) endorses the ascription to Gozzoli of the bulk of the angels in the *Christ in Glory*, and tentatively distributes the heads in the borders of the two fields between Giacomo da Poli and Giovanni d'Antonio.

SCENES FROM THE LIFE OF CHRIST. Museo di San Marco, Florence.   PLATES 123–131. FIGS. XXIX, XXX.
Panel: each scene approximately 39 × 39 cm.

The thirty-five scenes were designed to decorate the doors of the silver chest in the church of the Santissima Annunziata. The earliest reference to the silver chest occurs about 1460 in the *Theotocon* of Fra Domenico da Corella (publ. Lami, *Deliciae Eruditorum*, xii, pp. 49–116):

> Sunt ubi cum variis argentea vasa figuris
>   Quae tegit interius picta tabella foris,

> Angelicus pictor quam finxerat, ante Iohannes
>   Nomine, non Iotto, non Cimabove minor,
> Quorum fama fuit Tyrrhenas clara per urbes,
>   Ut dulci Dantes ore poeta canit.

The panels are also ascribed to Angelico in the *Memoriale* of Albertini of 1510 (*Memoriale di molte statue e pitture della citta di Firenze fatto da Francesco Albertini prete*, Florence, 1863, p. 12: 'Li ornamenti della argenteria per mano di fra Iohanni'), in the *Libro di Antonio Billi* of 1516–25/30 (p. 18: 'Nell' ornamento, doue stanno gli arienti, alla Nunziata de Seruj figure picole') and, between 1482 and 1497, by Manetti (p. 166: 'quasi tutto el tabernacolo degli arienti della Nunziata de' Servi').

The work is noted by Vasari (ii, pp. 511–12): 'Nella cappella similmente della Nunziata di Firenze, che fece fare Piero di Cosimo de' Medici, dipinse gli sportelli dell'armario, dove stanno l'argenterie, di figure piccole, condotte con molta diligenza.' The chest originally stood in the small oratory beside the chapel built by Michelozzo to the left of the main entrance of the church. Later the panels were shown in the Chiostrino dell'Antiporto; in 1687 they were replaced in the Cappella Feroni inside the church, and were subsequently moved to the Cappella dei Galli (1691). Details of the movements of the panels are given by Baldinucci (*Notizie de' Professori del Diseguo*, iii, 1768, pp. 90–1): 'Dipinse egli per la Cappella della Santissima Nunziata di Firenze, che fece fare Cosimo de' Medici, i portelli di un grande Armario nella facciata a man dritta entrando in essa Capella, dove stavano anticamente le argenterie, che agli anni addietro fu levato, e posto in quel luogo un molto devoto Croci-fisso di legno. . . . I detti portelli tutti storiati di piccole figure, della Vita, Morte e Resurrezione del Salvatore, furono da' Frati di quel Convento posti nel Chiostro piccolo, che e avanti alla Chiesa, credo io affine di esporlo a maggior venerazione de' popoli, e renderlo anche a' medesimi più godibile; ma non so già con quanta speranza di maggior durata, per esser quel luogo assai sottoposto all'ingiurie del tempo. Il che avendo osservato il Serenissimo Granduca Cosimo III mio Signore, operò che fossero tolti via, e collocati in più venerabile e più durevol posto, che fu per entro la chiesa medesima, da uno de' lati della Cappella de' cinque Santi, dico dalla parte di verso il maggiore Altare.' In 1785 the panels were moved to the Library, and thence to the Acca-demia (Paatz, i, p. 185). The subjects of the panels are scenes from the life of Christ (each accompanied by parallel quotations from the Old and New Testament), to which are added the scenes of Pentecost, the Coronation of the Virgin and the Last Judgment. The series is prefaced by a panel of *The Vision of Ezekiel* and concluded by the so-called *Lex Amoris*; a brief account of the iconography of these scenes is given in the Introduction to the present book.

There is some doubt as to the original form of the doors. The height of these was almost certainly coterminous with the height of the panels (118 cm.), each of which contains three tiers of scenes. The most plausible reconstruction is that of Douglas (pp. 119–20), who suggests that the panels decorated a single and a double door of the chest. They would thus be divisible into four groups:

(A) A single door composed of three rows of three panels and comprising the nine scenes from *The Vision of Ezekiel* to *Christ teaching in the Temple*.

(B) Three panels (*The Marriage at Cana*, *The Baptism of Christ* and *The Transfiguration*), which would have filled the space between this and the double door.

(C) A door composed of three rows of four panels and comprising the twelve scenes between *The Raising of Lazarus* and *The Flagellation* (Figs. XXIX, XXX).

(D) A door composed of three rows of four panels, comprising the eleven scenes between *Christ bearing the Cross* and *The Creed and Sacraments* and including the double scene of *The Last Judgment*.

Within each group the narrative ran from left to right.

The panels are generally assumed to have been commissioned by Piero de' Medici in 1448 (*Cronaca di Firenze di Benedetto Dei*, Bibl. Naz., Florence, Cod. Magl. xxi, f. 96 t.). A document published by Kennedy (*Alesso Baldovinetti*, 1938, p. 207), recording a payment for the hinges of the cupboard, shows that this was still unfinished in 1461. A further payment of February 1462 probably refers to the completion of the chest, and not, as assumed by D'Ancona (p. 82), to its repair.

All of the panels have been weakened by retouching. The extent of restoration can be gauged with comparison with photographs made prior to 1858 (Pls. 124, 129, 131). These show that in *The Annunciation* panel the angel's head, the lower part of the angel's hair, and his left upper arm, forearm and left hand are, in their present form, due to restoration. The expression of the Virgin's face has also been modified. There is extensive local restoration elsewhere on the panel. In the case of *The Adoration of the Magi* a large number of worm holes has been stippled in, and the heads of the figures on the left and of the kneeling King have been weakened by retouching, while the head of the Virgin has been rounded and softened. The most seriously damaged panel is *The Massacre of the Innocents*, in which retouching has gravely impaired the figures of Herod and of the women and soldiers beneath; in its present state this panel retains little of its original vitality.

From the time of Rio (*De l'art chrétien*, ii, p. 374) it has been observed that the panels of the chest are unequal in conception and in execution. Views on the authorship of the chest vary between the poles of Berenson (1932, p. 20), who accepts all of the panels save *The Marriage at Cana*, *The Baptism*, *The Transfiguration*, *The Vision of Ezekiel* and the *Lex Amoris* as substantially by Fra Angelico, and Muratoff (pp. 62–3), who discounts the possibility of Fra Angelico's intervention in or general responsibility for any of the scenes. In considering the authorship of the panels it is essential to remember first that they have been extensively restored, and secondly that those parts executed by Angelico are late works. With these points in mind it may be noted:

(i) The first nine scenes are so distinguished in conception and in such close conformity with the compositional methods of the San Marco predella as almost certainly to have been designed by the master. Angelico himself was certainly responsible for the execution of parts of *The Nativity*, *The Circumcision*, *The Adoration of the Magi*, *The Massacre of the Innocents*, the whole of *The Flight into Egypt* and *The Annunciation* and the figures in the much abraded *Christ teaching in the Temple*, and perhaps for all of the nine panels.

(ii) *The Marriage at Cana*, *The Baptism of Christ* and *The Transfiguration* are by Baldovinetti. The style of these three scenes depends from Domenico Veneziano rather than Angelico.

(iii) The remaining scenes are by a single hand wrongly identified by D'Ancona (p. 92) as that of the artist responsible for the frescoes of *Christ in Limbo*, *The Sermon on the Mount*, *The Arrest of Christ*, *The Agony in the Garden* and *The Institution of the Eucharist* in Cells 31–5 in the convent of San Marco. Four of the scenes (*The Raising of Lazarus*, *Christ's Entry into Jerusalem*, *The Last Supper* and *Judas receiving Payment*) may be generally dependent on cartoons by Angelico. The compositional schemes used in the remainder are totally dissimilar from those used by Angelico, except where they incorporate motifs from the San Marco frescoes. Examples of this are *The Mocking of Christ* (which derives from the corresponding fresco), *Christ carrying the Cross* (where the Virgin is based on the Virgin in the fresco), and *The Coronation of the Virgin* (where the central group is a reduced variant of that in Cell 9).

It is a reasonable hypothesis that the panels in group (i) were painted by Angelico in or soon after 1450, and that those in groups (ii) and (iii) were produced, in one case by Baldovinetti and in the other by the Master of Cell 2, between 1455 and 1461.

THE LAST JUDGMENT, THE ASCENSION AND PENTECOST. Galleria Nazionale (Corsini), Rome (No. 723). PLATE 132. FIG. XXXII. Panel: 54 × 74 cm.

From the Monte di Pietà. Doubt has been cast on the form of this painting, which is regarded by Crowe and Cavalcaselle (iv, 1911, p. 92) as 'altered in shape'. Schottmüller (p. 264) denies that the wings were originally part of the same complex as the central panel. The balance of evidence is that the painting was designed as a triptych in approximately its present form; the height of the central panel has, however, been reduced. The central panel is given by Muratoff (pl. cxi) to an assistant of Angelico, and is dismissed by Schottmüller (loc. cit.) as an inferior variant of the *Last Judgment* in Berlin (see below). When allowance is made for the condition of the painting, it is likely that all three panels were designed by the master, and that the central panel, at least, is substantially autograph. The attribution of the central panel to Angelico is admitted, among others, by Van Marle (x, pp. 133–4), who notes that it is superior in quality to the corresponding panel in Berlin, and by Berenson (1896, p. 100). The panel is certainly late in date, and Beissel (p. 120) assumes that it was executed at Santa Maria sopra Minerva. The Christ of the central panel is related to that of the *Last Judgment* in Berlin and repeats the pose utilized in the Orvieto fresco (q.v.), and the Christ of the right wing depends from the *Transfiguration* fresco at San Marco.

The Corsini *Last Judgment* is the only substantially autograph panel painting of this subject by Angelico. The following paintings of the *Last Judgment* have also been ascribed to the master:

(i) THE LAST JUDGMENT. Museo di San Marco, Florence.
Panel: 105 × 210 cm. FIG. XXXI.

From Santa Maria degli Angeli, Florence, where it is described by Vasari (ii, pp. 514–15): 'e nella chiesa de' monaci degli Angeli, un Paradiso ed un Inferno di figure piccole: nel quale con bella osservanza fece i beati bellissimi e pieni di giubbilo e di celeste letizia; ed i dannati, apparecchiati alle pene dell'Inferno, in varie guise mestissimi, e portanti nel volto impresso il peccato e demerito loro: i Beati si veggiono entrare celestemente ballando per la porta del paradiso; ed i dannati dai demonj all'inferno nelle eterne pene strascinati. Questa opera è in detta chiesa andando verso l'altar maggiore a man ritta, dove sta il sacerdote, quando si cantano la messa a sedere.' The concluding sentence is explained by Marchese (i, p. 279) as meaning that the painting occupied a position over the seat used by the priest during the celebration of high mass. The panel is listed by Manetti (p. 166), by Albertini (*Memoriale di molte statue e pitture della citta di Firenze fatto da Francesco Albertini, prete*, Florence, 1863, p. 13: 'uno Iuditio di fra Iohanni') and in the

XXIX. MASTER OF CELL 2 (?): SIX SCENES FROM THE LIFE OF CHRIST. Museo di San Marco, Florence.

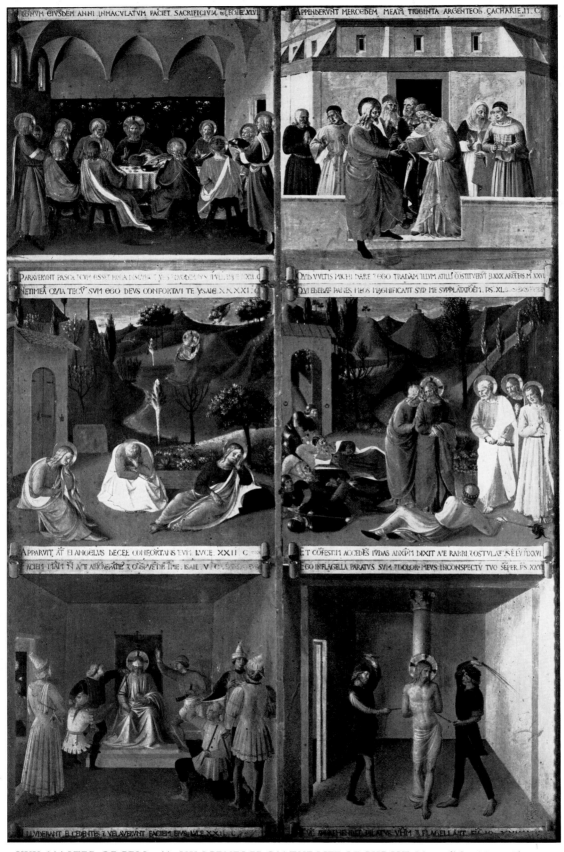

XXX. MASTER OF CELL 2 (?): SIX SCENES FROM THE LIFE OF CHRIST. Museo di San Marco, Florence.

XXXI. ZANOBI STROZZI: THE LAST JUDGMENT. Museo di San Marco, Florence.

XXXII. FRA ANGELICO: THE LAST JUDGMENT, THE ASCENSION AND PENTECOST. Galleria Corsini, Rome.

Libro di Antonio Billi of 1516–25/30 (p. 20: 'Negli Agnolj, cioe nel munistero uno inferno et paradiso'). The painting was later in the Cappella Segni (Paatz, iii, p. 137), and was subsequently transferred to the Accademia, and thence to San Marco.

The panel is regarded by Douglas (pp. 58–61) as an early work of Angelico painted immediately before the Santa Maria Nuova *Coronation of the Virgin*. Berenson (1909, p. 105) accepts the attribution to Angelico with the proviso that the section on the right was executed by another hand. Muratoff (pp. 34–5), proposing a dating between 1420 and 1430, suggests that the panel was begun by Angelico and completed by a pupil, and Van Marle (x, p. 170) and Bazin (p. 184) presume that it was largely executed by a pupil working from Angelico's cartoon. Van Marle identifies this pupil with Zanobi Strozzi, and Schottmüller (p. 257) with the artist of the National Gallery predella. Wurm (p. 60) denies Angelico's authorship of the panel.

In terms of iconography, the *Last Judgment* was one of Angelico's most popular inventions. The present painting is based either on a cartoon by Angelico or on a lost prototype. The presence, in Giovanni di Paolo's *Paradiso* in the Metropolitan Museum, New York, and his *Last Judgment* in the Pinacoteca at Siena, of motifs which seem to derive from Fra Angelico but cannot be referred to any of Angelico's surviving paintings, lends some colour to the view that the Santa Maria degli Angeli panel derives from a superior autograph work. There is no reason to believe that any part of the Santa Maria degli Angeli painting, as it at present stands, was executed by Angelico, and the weak, diffused design, with its uncertain space relationships, has more of the character of a free variant than of a faithful transcription from a cartoon by the artist. The upper section in particular has clearly been adapted from a rectangular scheme to conform to the irregular shape of the arched panel. Here the relation of the panel to its original must have been analogous to that between the Santa Maria Nuova *Coronation of the Virgin* in the Uffizi and the altarpiece of the same subject in the Louvre. The panel (which is by the presumed Zanobi Strozzi and was executed about 1435–40) none the less gives a more faithful impression than other variants of the character of Angelico's lost prototype.

Detail from Fig. XXXII

XXXIII. ZANOBI STROZZI: THE LAST JUDGMENT. Kaiser Friedrich Museum, Berlin.

(ii) THE LAST JUDGMENT. Kaiser Friedrich Museum, Berlin (No. 60A). FIG. XXXIII.

Panel: (centre) 101×63 cm., (wings) 101×27 cm.

Coll.: a baker in Rome (1811); Cardinal Fesch (soon after 1816); Fesch sale (1845); Prince Musignano; Lord Ward (Earl of Dudley); purchased for Kaiser Friedrich Museum, 1884.

Originally painted on a single panel, probably of the same dimensions (116×148 cm.) and certainly of the same proportions as a copy made by Spranger in 1567 for Pope Pius V, now in Turin. The panel is given to Angelico, *inter alios*, by Douglas (p. 132), Schottmüller (p. 264) and Berenson (1896, p. 98). Except by Muratoff (p. 36), who links it with the Santa Maria degli Angeli *Last Judgment*, it is generally regarded as a late work, dating from Angelico's first Roman period and therefore roughly contemporary with the Orvieto frescoes. The cartoon of the Christ is closely related to that of the corresponding figure at Orvieto, and if, as is likely, the panel depends from the fresco, it must have been produced about 1448. The handling throughout is strongly reminiscent of that of the Montecarlo *Annunciation* of about 1445, and the painting is almost certainly a later work by the same artist. According to the catalogue of the Kaiser Friedrich Museum (*Beschreibendes Verzeichnis der Gemälde im Kaiser-Friedrich-Museum und Deutschen Museum*, 1931, p. 18), a weak and overpainted copy of the Berlin *Last Judgment* appeared for sale in Rome in 1914. This was stated to have come from the church of the Cappuccini at Leonforte (near Catania) and was owned by Baron Lidestri di Artesinella. This painting (also described by Douglas, p. 199) is untraced.

CHRIST ON THE CROSS BETWEEN THE VIRGIN AND SAINT JOHN WITH A DOMINICAN CARDINAL. Fogg Art Museum, Cambridge (Mass.).

Dimensions: 88×36 cm. PLATE 133. FIG. 13.

Coll.: Timbal (bt. Bologna 1860); Prof. Noel Valois; Hervey E. Wetzel. Valois ('Fra Angelico et le Cardinal Jean de Torquemada', in *Société Nationale des Antiquaires de France, Centenaire 1804–1904: Recueil de Mémoires*, 1904, pp. 461–70) identifies the donor's portrait as that of the Spanish Dominican Juan de Torquemada, who was born in 1388, was created cardinal in 1439 and died in 1468. This identification is supported by the presence of a cardinal's hat in front of the kneeling figure, and by comparison with a later portrait of Juan de Torquemada included in the *Annunciation* of Antoniasso Romano in Santa Maria sopra Minerva. The panel is accepted as a work of Angelico by Berenson (1909, p. 107), Muratoff (p. 65) and most other students of Angelico, and is ascribed by Borenius ('A Fra Angelico for Harvard', in *Burlington Magazine*, xxxix, 1921, pp. 209–10) to the years 1449–53. It finds a point of reference in the autograph panels of the Annunziata silver chest.

OTHER WORKS ASCRIBED TO FRA ANGELICO

I
PAINTINGS

AMSTERDAM, Rijksmuseum (No. 17A). *Madonna and Child*. Panel: 74×61 cm. Coll.: Quadt (till 1869); Augusteum, Oldenburg (till 1923).

Ascribed to Angelico by Bode (in *Catalogus van den Jubileum Tentoonstelling in der Rijksmuseum te Amsterdam*, 1923, No. 156), Schottmüller (1924, pp. 102, 261), A. Venturi (*Studi dal Vero*, 1927, p. 11), Berenson (1932, p. 19), Van Marle (x, p. 138) and other critics. If, as is likely, the pose of the Child derives from the Bosco ai Frati altarpiece in the Museo di San Marco, the panel can hardly date before 1440–5, and was possibly painted under the supervision of Angelico.

BERLIN, Kaiser Friedrich Museum (No. 60). *Madonna Child and with Saints Dominic and Peter Martyr*.   FIG. XXXIV.
Panel: 70×51 cm. Coll.: Solly (1821).

Ascribed to Angelico by Crowe and Cavalcaselle (iv, p. 93), Berenson (1896, p. 98), Schottmüller (1924, p. 260) and Muratoff (p. 36). Attribution questioned by Van Marle (x, p. 140). The form of the Virgin's head has been modified by restoration, but the type of the Child is closely related to that in the Parma *Madonna* (q.v.), and both panels appear to have been painted about 1430 in the workshop of Angelico.

XXXIV. Workshop of FRA ANGELICO: VIRGIN AND CHILD WITH SAINTS DOMINIC AND PETER MARTYR. Kaiser Friedrich Museum, Berlin.

★BOSTON, Museum of Fine Arts (No. 14.416). *Madonna and Child enthroned with Saints Peter, Paul and George, four Angels and a Donor*.
Panel: 25×25 cm. Coll.: Aynard, Lyons (sale 1913, No. 33).

Berenson (1932, p. 20) as Angelico; Van Marle (x, p. 156) and Muratoff (pl. cclviii) as workshop of Angelico. Possibly an early work by the author of a number of *Madonnas* published by Berenson ('Quadri senza Casa', in *Dedalo*, xii, 1932, pp. 523–9) as Domenico di Michelino, here referred to as the Pseudo-Domenico di Michelino.

★BOSTON, Isabella Stewart Gardner Museum. *The Burial and Assumption of the Virgin*. See FLORENCE, Museo di San Marco (pp. 199–200).

★CLEVELAND, Museum of Art. *The Coronation of the Virgin*. Panel: 27×37 cm.

Coll.: Contini-Bonacossi; Elisabeth Severance Prentiss. Stated to have been ascribed to Angelico by Swarzenski, Mather, Mayer and Longhi, the latter with a dating ca. 1425–30. Close in style to Arcangelo di Cola da Camerino.

★DETROIT, Mrs Edsel Ford. *Annunciatory Angel* and *Virgin Annunciate*.   FIG. XXXVI.
Panel: 36×26 cm. (each). Coll.: Duke of Hamilton; J. E. Taylor; Sedelmeyer; Carl Hamilton.

Ascribed to Angelico by Berenson (1932, p. 20), Van Marle (x, p. 143), L. Venturi (*Italian Paintings in America*, 1933, Nos. 176, 177) and most other critics. The panels seem to have formed the lateral pinnacles of an altarpiece, perhaps *The Coronation of the Virgin* in the Louvre, where the tooled haloes of a number of the angels in the upper part of the panel are closely similar.

FLORENCE, Museo di San Marco. *Madonna and Child enthroned*.   FIG. 2
Panel: 189×81 cm.

Provenance unknown. In the left hand of the Child is a cartellino with the words:
.DISCITE AME QVIA MITIS SVM Z. VMILIS CORDE
Z.INVENIETIS REQVIEM ANIMABVS VESTRIS.
The painting formed the central panel of a polyptych. As pointed out by Schottmüller (p. 227), its scheme is generically related to that of the Monte Oliveto altarpiece of Lorenzo Monaco of 1406–10, now in the Uffizi, and on this account it is generally regarded as Angelico's earliest surviving work, Muratoff (p. 27) proposing a dating about 1420 and Schottmüller (p. 1) placing it in the bracket 1425–30. Longhi (1928–9, p. 155) alone advances a dating after 1430. The treatment is conspicuously less Gothic than that of the central panel of the altarpiece in San Domenico at Fiesole, and the earliest admissible date is thus about 1430–33. A derivative from Lorenzo Monaco's polyptych is found in the Prato altarpiece of Andrea di Giusto as late as 1435. Berenson (1909, p. 105) notes that the *Trinity* in the upper part of the frame is not by Angelico; the ascription of this part of the painting to Angelico is accepted by Salmi (1950, p. 78). The figures of the Virgin and Child are substantially autograph.

FLORENCE, Museo di San Marco. *Madonna and Child with Saints Dominic, John the Baptist, Peter Martyr and Thomas Aquinas*.
Panel: 137×168 cm.   FIG. XXXV.

From San Pietro Martire, Florence. Listed by Vasari (ii, pp. 515–6): 'Alle monache di San Pietro martire, che oggi stanno nel monastero di San Felice in piazza, il quale era dell'ordine di Camaldoli, fece in una tavola la Nostra Donna, San Giovan Battista, San Domenico, San Tommaso, e San Pietro martire, con figure piccole assai.' The altarpiece was moved to San Felice in 1557 (Paatz, ii, pp. 51, 56). Van Marle (x, p. 42) as an early work of Angelico, Berenson (1932, p. 20) and most other critics as workshop of Angelico. The main panels of the triptych are so

XXXV. FRA ANGELICO (?): VIRGIN AND CHILD WITH SAINTS DOMINIC, JOHN THE BAPTIST, PETER
MARTYR AND THOMAS AQUINAS. Museo di San Marco, Florence.

XXXVI. FRA ANGELICO (?): THE ANNUNCIATORY ANGEL AND VIRGIN ANNUNCIATE. Mrs. Edsel Ford, Detroit.

paramenta faciens in sacristia et plures reliquias sanctorum adornavit.' The reliquary panels are also mentioned by Vasari (ii, p. 513): 'e in Santa Maria Novella, oltre alle cose dette, dipinse di storie piccole il cereo pasquale, ed alcuni reliquieri che nelle maggiori solennità si pongono in sull'altare.' The other three reliquary panels are presumed to be:

(i) *The Annunciation and Adoration of the Magi.* Museo di San Marco, Florence.   FIG. XXXVIII.
Panel: 42×25 cm.

(ii) *The Coronation of the Virgin.* Museo di San Marco. Florence.
Panel: 42×25 cm.   FIG. XXXIX.

(iii) *The Burial and Assumption of the Virgin.* Isabella Stewart Gardner Museum, Boston.   FIG. XL.
Panel: 58×36 cm.

The four panels are recorded by Richa (iii, 1754, p. 49) in the sacristy of Santa Maria Novella. Three of them (the *Madonna della Stella* and those listed as (i) and (ii) above) were seen by Milanesi (in Vasari, ii, p. 514 n.) in a reliquary cupboard in Santa Maria Novella, and were transferred in 1868 to San Marco. The Boston panel was purchased in the first half of the nineteenth century by the Rev. John Sanford, and bequeathed by him in 1857 to Lord Methuen; it was sold through Colnaghi to Mrs Gardner in 1899. Waagen (*Galleries and Cabinets of Art in Great Britain*, 1857, p. 397) states that the panel was 'formerly the altarpiece of a chapel near Leghorn'. Despite this indication, there is a high degree of probability that this panel belongs with those now at San Marco. All four panels are accepted as works of Angelico by Berenson (1909, pp. 104–5). Some measure of studio intervention is presumed by other students. The *Madonna della Stella* is given to Angelico by

XXXVII. ZANOBI STROZZI: MADONNA DELLA STELLA. Museo di San Marco, Florence.

heavily repainted that their authorship cannot be established; it is possible that they were painted by Angelico about 1425. Salmi (1950, p. 154) regards the narrative scenes above the finials as later additions to the altarpiece by Gozzoli.

FLORENCE, Museo di San Marco. *Madonna della Stella.*
Panel: 60×30 cm.   FIG. XXXVII.

The painting is one of four reliquary panels formerly preserved in Santa Maria Novella. The attribution of these panels to Angelico goes back to a passage in the *Chronaca* of Biliotti of 1570–1600 (xix, p. 24, quoted by Marchese, i, p. 270): 'Habemus et multas plurimorum Sanctorum reliquias, quas quidem fr. Joannes Masius fiorentinus, multae devotionis et taciturnitatis vir, in quatuor inclusit tabellas, quae fr. Joannes fesolanus pictor, cognomento Angelicus, pulcherrimis beatissimae Mariae Virginis et Sanctorum Angelorum ornavit figuris. Obiit fr. Joannes Masius anno 1430.' The latter date is qualified by Marchese with the gloss: 'Nel manoscritto si legge veramente 1333, ma deb' essere un errore di penna.' An entry in the *Necrologio* of Santa Maria Novella (f. 58 n.) reveals that Fra Giovanni Masi in fact died in 1434: 'N.603. Fr. Johannes Masi obiit florentie die 27 junij 1434. hic fuit maxime devotionis vir ad unguem regularem vitam servavit quoad omnia sed potissime quoad silentium fuit enim supra modum taciturnus et tam magnus et assiduus confessor quod ex assiduitate maxima plures intraret egritudines . . . hic plurima de suis patrimonialibus

XXXVIII. ZANOBI STROZZI: THE ANNUNCIATION AND ADORATION OF THE MAGI.
Museo di San Marco, Florence.

XXXIX. ZANOBI STROZZI: THE CORONATION
OF THE VIRGIN. Museo di San Marco, Florence.

XL. ZANOBI STROZZI: THE BURIAL AND ASSUMP-
TION OF THE VIRGIN. Gardner Museum, Boston.

all critics save Wurm (p. 7), and the *Annunciation and Adoration of the Magi* is accepted by Douglas (p. 35), Schottmüller (p. 257), Van Marle (x, p. 46), Papini (p. 15), Muratoff (pp. 29–30) and Bazin (p. 181). The Boston panel is accepted by Douglas (pp. 37–8), Schottmüller (p. 256) and Hendy (*The Isabella Stewart Gardner Museum: Catalogue of the Exhibited Paintings and Drawings*, 1931, pp. 10–13), and rejected by Wurm (pp. 6–7), Van Marle (x, pp. 46, 148), Muratoff (Pls. xlii, xliii) and Bazin (p. 181). Van Marle advances a tentative ascription for this panel to Zanobi Strozzi, and Wurm and Muratoff ascribe it to the artist responsible for the predella panels of *The Marriage and Burial of the Virgin* in the Museo di San Marco. The *Coronation of the Virgin* is denied to Angelico by Douglas (pp. 38–43), Schottmüller (pp. 267–8), Van Marle (x, p. 46), Muratoff (pls. xli, xlii) and Bazin (p. 181). The statement of Biliotti that the four panels were commissioned by Fra Giovanni Masi has led most writers on Angelico to date them before his presumed death in 1430. Since the *Annunciation* depends from the Cortona altarpiece, and the *Coronation of the Virgin* from the painting in the Louvre, this early dating is untenable, and the four panels can hardly have been executed before 1435–40. The weak, miniature-like handling and inadequate spatial definition of the three narrative panels link them to the Santa Maria Nuova *Coronation of the Virgin* in the Uffizi. Muratoff suggests that the discrepancies between the type of the Virgin in the *Madonna della Stella* and comparable figures in the autograph paintings of Angelico are due to restoration. Examination of the surface of the panel does not substantiate this view, and there can be no reasonable doubt that the figure was executed by the same hand as the three other panels. All four panels are by Zanobi Strozzi.

FORLI, Pinacoteca. *The Nativity* and *The Agony in the Garden*. Panel: 26 × 16 cm. each.   FIGS. XLI, XLII.
Associated with the workshop of Angelico by Schottmüller (1924, p. 241) and other critics, and republished by Longhi (p. 176) as autograph early works datable before 1430. The compositions of the two panels are not consistent with those employed elsewhere by Angelico, and the scheme of *The Agony in the Garden*, with a reclining apostle in the front plane, suggests the influence of *The Transfiguration* at San Marco and certain of the panels of the Annunziata silver chest. The two scenes are of high quality.

LEGHORN, Santa Maria del Soccorso. *Christ crowned with Thorns*.
Panel: 55 × 39 cm.
Longhi (1928–9, pp. 153–9) as Angelico. This attribution is not convincing.

★LENINGRAD, Hermitage. *Madonna and Child with four Angels*.
Panel. Coll.: Stroganoff.
A. Venturi ('Quadri di Gentile da Fabriano a Milano e a Pietroburgo', in *L'Arte*, i, 1898, p. 495) as Gentile da Fabriano; Colasanti ('Nuovi dipinti di Arcangelo di Cola da Camerino,' in *Bollettino d'Arte*, ser. ii, I, 1921–2, pp. 544–5) as Arcangelo di Cola; Longhi (1928–9, p. 154, and 1940, p. 186) and Salmi (1950, p. 78) as Angelico. The attribution to Angelico, which is inseparable from that of the *Madonna* at Vierhouten (see p. 204), is based on alleged resemblances to the Fiesole altarpiece, and involves a dating about 1425.

XLI. Workshop of FRA ANGELICO: THE NATIVITY.
Pinacoteca, Forli.

XLII. Workshop of FRA ANGELICO: THE AGONY IN
THE GARDEN. Pinacoteca, Forli.

LONDON, National Gallery (No. 5581). *Madonna and Child with nine Angels.*
Panel: 29×22 cm. Coll.: Miss Rogers (prior to 1844); Samuel Rogers (sale 1856, 2 May, lot 614); C. S. Bale (sale 1881, 14 May, lot 290); Cook (till 1945).

Variously regarded as an early work by Fra Angelico of 1425–30 (Longhi, pp. 174–5), an early work by Benozzo Gozzoli (Cook catalogue, 1932, and earlier), a putative early work by Domenico Veneziano (Berenson, 1932, p. 172) and an early work by Boccatis (Douglas, in *L'Arte*, 1903, p. 108). None of these attributions is satisfactory.

LONDON, National Gallery (No. 2908). *A Martyr Bishop.*
Panel: 14 cm. diameter. Coll.: Lady Lindsay (prior to 1893); Lady Lindsay Bequest (1912).

As suggested by Davies (*National Gallery Catalogues: The Earlier Italian Schools*, 1951, pp. 24–5), this panel probably formed part of the framing of an altarpiece, and was produced in the workshop of Angelico. A similar panel in the collection of Mr Henry L. Moses, New York (listed by Berenson, 1932, as Angelico) was formerly in the Samuel Rogers collection, and is said to originate from an altarpiece in San Domenico, Fiesole.

LONDON, H.M. the Queen. *St Peter Martyr.*
Panel: 26×8.5 cm. Coll.: Metzger (1845).

Berenson (1932, p. 22) as Angelico. Pilaster panel from an unidentified altarpiece, possibly autograph.

LONDON, H.M. the Queen. *Christ blessing.*
Panel: 28×22.5 cm. Coll.: Spence (1854).

Berenson (1532, p. 22) as Angelico. By Zanobi Strozzi.

★LUGANO, Thyssen Foundation. *Madonna and Child with five Angels.* FIG. XLIV.

Panel: 100×49 cm. Coll.: Palazzo Gondi, Florence; King of the Belgians; Kleinberger, Paris (1909); Pierpont Morgan.

A direct ascription to Angelico is advanced by A. Venturi (in *L'Arte*, xii, 1909, pp. 319–20), Schottmüller (p. 234), Muratoff (pl. cxxviii) and Berenson (1932, p. 22). Van Marle (x, pp. 139–40), who questions the attribution to Angelico, proposes an ascription to Benozzo Gozzoli. As pointed out by Collobi-Ragghianti ('Zanobi Strozzi-II', in *La Critica d'Arte*, xxxiii, 1950, p. 25), the angels in a *Madonna and Child with four Angels* at Bergamo are imitated from those in this painting. The design is consistent with a dating about 1445–50. The composition of a (much repainted) *Madonna and Child with two Angels* in the collection of the Duke of Alba recalls that of the upper section of the Thyssen panel.

★NEW YORK, Metropolitan Museum (No. 14.40.628). *Christ on the Cross with the Virgin and Saints Monica, Augustine, Dominic, Mary Magdalen, John the Evangelist, Thomas Aquinas, Francis and Elisabeth of Hungary.* FIG. XLV.
Panel: 40×54 cm. Coll.: Gouvello de Kériaval, Paris; Benjamin Altman, New York.

Crowe and Cavalcaselle (iv, p. 97 n.) and Berenson (1932, p. 22) as a ruined work by Fra Angelico, Van Marle (x, p. 160) as a shop piece. In 1951 the panel was cleaned, and repaint removed from the heads; a modern landscape background was also erased. The widely spaced figures recall the practice of the Master of Cell 36.

XLIII

XLIV

XLV

XLIII. Workshop of FRA ANGELICO: THE REDEEMER.
Museo di San Matteo, Pisa.

XLIV. Workshop of FRA ANGELICO: VIRGIN AND
CHILD WITH FOUR ANGELS. Thyssen Foundation, Lugano.

XLV. Workshop of FRA ANGELICO: CHRIST ON THE
CROSS WITH THE VIRGIN AND EIGHT SAINTS.
Metropolitan Museum, New York.

XLVI. Workshop of FRA ANGELICO: VIRGIN AND CHILD WITH SAINTS JOHN THE BAPTIST, DOMINIC, FRANCIS AND PAUL. Pinacoteca, Parma.

PARIS, Louvre (No. 1294B). *Angel.*
Panel: 38×26 cm. Coll.: Gay.

Schottmüller (p. 240), Berenson (1932, p. 22) and Van Marle (x, p. 58) as Angelico. From the workshop of Angelico. According to Van Marle, a similar angel, supposed to have formed part of the tabernacle in San Domenico at Fiesole, is in the Thierry de la Noue collection.

PARMA, Pinacoteca (No. 429). *Madonna and Child with Saints John the Baptist, Dominic, Francis and Paul.*   FIG. XLVI.
Panel: 101×56 cm. Acquired in Florence in 1787 by Tacoli Canacci; bought for the Parma Gallery from the heirs of Dr Giuseppe Campanini (1842).

A direct ascription to Angelico is sustained by Berenson (1896. p. 100), Van Marle (x, p. 58), and Schottmüller (p. 230), and is questioned by Crowe and Cavalcaselle (iv, p. 93), Douglas (p. 197) and Muratoff (pp. 32–3). The four kneeling figures in the foreground are by Zanobi Strozzi, but the group of the Virgin and Child in the upper part of the panel is almost certainly based on a cartoon by Angelico of about 1430, and may have been executed by the master. A predella with figures of Saints Nicholas, Lawrence and Peter Martyr in the Kunstmuseum at Berne (No. 847) is associated by Collobi-Ragghianti ('Zanobi Strozzi – I', in *La Critica d'Arte*, xxxii, 1950, p. 468) with this painting.

PISA, Museo di San Matteo. *The Redeemer.*   FIG. XLIII.
Linen: 193×78 cm.

Berenson (1896, p. 100) as Angelico; Schottmüller (p. 219) and Van Marle (x, p. 162) as school of Angelico. Workshop of Angelico.

★PRINCETON, University Gallery. *The Virgin* and *Saint John the Evangelist.*
Panel: 29×13 cm.

Mather ('Two unpublished Fra Angelicos', in *Art in America*, xxii, 1934, pp. 92–5) and Berenson (1936, p. 20) as Angelico; Salmi (1950, p. 149) as Battista di Biagio Sanguigni. The two panels seem to have formed the wings of a *Crucifixion* triptych, and are late works by Zanobi Strozzi.

TURIN, Pinacoteca Sabauda. *Madonna and Child.*
Panel: 100×60 cm. Coll.: Prince Michael Boutourlin; Sandrini; Garrod (till 1852).

Denied to Angelico by Crowe and Cavalcaselle (iv, p. 93 n.), Beissel (p. 61) and Muratoff (p. 42), and omitted from the Angelico catalogue of Berenson. An attribution to Angelico is sustained by Schottmüller (p. 90) and Salmi (p. 81), who relates the pose of the Child to that shown in a miniature of about 1434 by Belbello da Pavia in the Vatican. The architectural background of the panel is Lippesque, but the forms in the two figures derive from Angelico, and the type of the Child recalls that employed in the Perugia polyptych.

TURIN, Pinacoteca Sabauda. *Two Angels.*
Panel: 25×13 cm. (each). Coll.: Metzger; Garrod (till 1846).

The two panels seem to have formed part of a frame. Schottmüller (p. 24), Berenson (1896, p. 100) and Van Marle (x, p. 46) as Angelico. Workshop of Angelico.

XLVII. ZANOBI STROZZI: VIRGIN AND CHILD ENTHRONED WITH NINE ANGELS AND SAINTS DOMINIC AND CATHERINE OF ALEXANDRIA. Pinacoteca Vaticana.

VATICAN CITY, Pinacoteca Vaticana (No. 253). *Madonna and Child enthroned with nine Angels and Saints Dominic and Catherine of Alexandria.*   FIG. XLVII.
Panel: 23 × 18 cm. Coll.: Bisenzio (Rome); Earl of Dudley (till 1877).

Given unanimously to Angelico. Muratoff (pl. xxxix) places the panel about 1425, and Schottmüller (p. 228) and Van Marle (x, p. 58) note that the composition depends from that of the central panel of the polyptych at Fiesole. The type of the Child reflects that in the Annalena and Pontassieve *Madonnas*, and the panel can thus hardly have been painted before 1438–40. The handling is characteristic of Zanobi Strozzi.

★VIERHOUTEN, D. G. van Beuningen. *Madonna and Child with two Angels.*   FIG. XLVIII.
Panel: 81 × 47 cm. Coll.: Cassirer, Berlin.

Colasanti ('Nuovi dipinti di Arcangelo di Cola da Camerino', in *Bollettino d'Arte*, ser. ii, I, 1921–2, pp. 539–40) and Berenson ('Quadri senza Casa', in *Dedalo*, x, 1929, pp. 136, 140, and 1936, p. 28) as Arcangelo di Cola; Gronau (verbally), Longhi (1928–9, pp. 154–5, and 1940, p. 186) and Salmi (1950, p. 78) as Angelico. The attribution to Angelico involves a dating in the early or mid-twenties. The problem of authorship is inseparable from that of the authorship of the *Madonna* at Leningrad (see p. 200). Both paintings are perhaps by Arcangelo di Cola.

WASHINGTON, National Gallery of Art (Kress collection). *The Adoration of the Magi.*
Panel: 133 cm. (diameter). Coll.: William Coningham (sale 1849); Alexander Barker (sale 1874); Cook.

Generally ascribed to Fra Filippo Lippi until, in 1932, the thesis was advanced by Berenson ('Fra Angelico, Fra Filippo e la crono-logia', in *Bollettino d'Arte*, xxvi, 1932–3, pp. 1 and 49 ff.) that the panel was begun by Fra Angelico, and completed, about 1445, by Lippi. This case is sustained by Suida (in *Paintings and Drawings from the Kress Collection*, 1951, p. 42), who follows Pudelko in identifying the panel with a tondo of the same subject ascribed in the Medici inventory of 1492 to Angelico. Lippi's authorship is reaffirmed by Pudelko ('Per la datazione delle opere di Fra Filippo Lippi', in *Rivista d'Arte*, 1936, xviii, p. 68) and Oertel (*Fra Filippo Lippi*, 1942, p. 70), the latter with a dating ca. 1455–7. The tondo is substantially by Fra Filippo Lippi.

★WASHINGTON, National Gallery of Art (Kress collection). *The Lamentation over the Dead Christ.*
Panel: 89 × 55 cm. Coll.: Bardini, Florence; Goldman, New York.

The ascription of this much repainted panel to Angelico is due to Schottmüller (1924, p. 266) and Berenson (1932, p. 22), by whom it is regarded as a late work. Schottmüller presumes the interven-tion of Pesellino. Angelico's authorship of the panel is questioned by Van Marle (x, p. 143) and Ragghianti ('La collezione Kress della National Gallery of Art di Washington', in *La Critica d'Arte*, xxvii, 1949, p. 81), who suggests, on the analogy of the Washington tondo, that the panel was begun by Angelico and completed by Fra Filippo Lippi. In certain details the scheme recalls that of the *Lamentation* on the Annunziata silver chest, but, so far as can be judged from detail photographs, neither design nor execution is due to Angelico.

★WASHINGTON, National Gallery of Art (Mellon collec-tion). *Madonna and Child with two Angels.*
Panel: 62 × 47 cm. Coll.: Steinkopff; Countess of Seaforth; Mellon.

Officially ascribed to Angelico, and presumed to have been painted about 1430–40 (*The National Gallery of Art: Preliminary Catalogue*

XLVIII. ARCANGELO DI COLA DA CAMERINO (?): VIRGIN AND CHILD ENTHRONED WITH TWO ANGELS (Mr D. G. van Beuningen, Vierhouten).

of Paintings and Sculpture, 1941, pp. 5–6). The painting is closely related in style to the Cosmas and Damian predella by Zanobi Strozzi in the Museo di San Marco.

★WIESBADEN, Henckell collection. *Madonna and Child with Saint Catherine of Alexandria and four Angels.*
Canvas (transferred from panel): 91 × 46 cm. Coll.: Barker; Earl of Dudley (sale 1892, 25 June, No. 39); Sedelmeyer, Paris; Schaeffer, Frankfurt-am-Main.

Noted by Waagen (*Treasures of Art in Great Britain*, ii, 1854, p. 231), and accepted as a work of Angelico by Crowe and Caval-caselle (iv, p. 93), Berenson (1909, p. 22; not subsequent editions), and Schottmüller (1924, p. 260). Presumed by Van Marle (x, pp. 138–40) to have been executed in large part by Gozzoli. The painting is related to the Berlin and Parma *Madonnas* (q.v.), and was probably produced in the workshop of Angelico.

II
DRAWINGS

BUFFALO, Albright Art Gallery.   FIG. XLIX.
Two Scenes from the Legend of a Holy Hermit.
Pen and ink, and water-colour on vellum: 25.4 × 13.6 cm.

This drawing (which forms part of the same series as a drawing in the Metropolitan Museum, New York) was lent to the 1930 Exhibition of Italian Art at the Royal Academy, London, from the Oppenheimer collection, along with one of two sections of a roll, dated 1417, illustrating the journey of a Dominican friar, Fra Pietro della Croce, to the Holy Land. The present drawing and the roll are regarded by Popham (*Italian Drawings exhibited at the Royal Academy, Burlington House, London*, 1931, Nos. 11, 12) as by a single hand. Clark ('Italian Drawings at Burlington House', in *Burlington Magazine*, lvi, 1930, p. 175) notes that 'the only painter with whose style they have anything in common seems to be Fra Angelico'. A direct ascription to Angelico is advanced by Longhi (p. 173).

CHANTILLY, Musée Condé.
Recto: Christ as Judge and two Angels: a kneeling Angel.
Verso: Head of a Monk.
Bistre wash heightened with white on buff prepared paper: 25 × 15.5 cm.

Schottmüller (p. xxxiii) as Angelico. As recognized by Berenson (*The Drawings of the Florentine Painters*, iii, 1938, No. 530, p.48), a characteristic sheet by Gozzoli. Douglas (p. 199) wrongly regards the *recto* as a study for the Corsini *Last Judgment*. Berenson (op. cit., i, p. 7, and iii, p. 48) connects the angel on the *recto* with the Orvieto *Last Judgment* and regards the *verso* tentatively as a portrait of Angelico. A connection with the Orvieto fresco is very possible.

XLIX. MASTER OF 1417: TWO SCENES FROM THE LEGEND OF A HOLY HERMIT. Albright Art Gallery, Buffalo.

L. After FRA ANGELICO: CHRIST ON THE CROSS.
Albertina, Vienna.

DRESDEN, Kupferstichkabinett.
Recto: Archangel (Saint Michael?) holding Sword and Globe: naked Putto.
Verso: Lion and naked Youth.
Bistre wash on white paper rubbed with red chalk: 24.5 × 14 cm.

Douglas (p. 199) and Schottmüller (p. xxxii) as Angelico. Berenson (op. cit., iii, No. 532, p. 48) as Gozzoli.

LONDON, British Museum (1895-9-15-437).
King David playing a Psaltery.
Pen and brown ink and purple wash on parchment: 19.7 × 17.9 cm.

Accepted as Angelico by almost all writers on the artist, and regarded by Berenson (op. cit., i, p. 4) as 'the only drawing by Fra Angelico which leaves no ground for doubt'. Popham (*Italian Drawings in the Department of Prints and Drawings in the British Museum: the Fourteenth and Fifteenth Centuries*, i, 1950, p. 2) points out that the drawing is on a piece of waste parchment, and is not necessarily a study for an illumination. The forms are closely related to those in the paintings ascribed throughout this volume to Zanobi Strozzi, and the study is almost certainly by this artist.

VIENNA, Albertina (S.R. 20).   FIG. L.
Christ on the Cross.
Bistre and red wash: 29 × 19 cm.

Douglas (p. 199) as a study for the fresco of *Christ on the Cross* in the upper corridor at San Marco. Berenson (op. cit., i, p. 4) as 'more probably by some unknown and charming imitator', rightly drawing attention to weaknesses in the folds of the loin-cloth which preclude Angelico's authorship.

III
MINIATURES

FLORENCE, Biblioteca Laurenziana. *Chorale No. 3*.
The miniatures in this volume from Santa Maria degli Angeli fall into two groups, one of which is correctly given by Ciaranfi ('Lorenzo Monaco miniatore', in *L'Arte*, n.s. iii, 1932, pp. 302–17) to Lorenzo Monaco, and the other assigned to a 'tendenza dell' Angelico' with the tentative suggestion that they may be the earliest known works of this artist. Salmi (1950, pp. 75–7) accepts the following illuminations as works by Angelico:

c. 1v.   *The Resurrection.*
c. 6v.   *Christ with two Apostles on the Road to Emmaus.*
c. 11r.   *Christ and the Apostles.*
c. 15r.   *The Elect contemplating the Redeemer.*
c. 23v.   *Christ and the Apostles.*
c. 41v.   *Choir of Monks.*

c. 57v.   *David dancing.*
c. 80v.   *Pentecost.*

Longhi (p. 163) assigns the miniatures not to the year inscribed on the volume (1409) but to after 1420, and regards them as the work of an unknown imitator of Angelico. The miniatures are not directly related to Angelico's authenticated early works.

FLORENCE, Museo di San Marco.
Four volumes in the Museo di San Marco (Nos. 16, 17, 19 and 44) are ascribed to Angelico by Wingenroth ('Beiträge zur Angelico-Forschung', in *Repertorium für Kunstwissenschaft*, xxi, 1898, pp. 343–5). This attribution is refuted by Douglas (pp. 180–1), and the volumes are given by D'Ancona (*La Miniatura Italiana*, ii, 1914, pp. 345–56) to Zanobi Strozzi. Wingenroth's contention is correct in so far as it presupposes an identity of authorship between these volumes and the reliquary panels in the Museo di San Marco ascribed to Fra Angelico, and the volumes afford contributory evidence of Zanobi Strozzi's responsibility for these and other related panel paintings.

LOST WORKS BY FRA ANGELICO

FLORENCE, Badia. *Saint Benedict.*
A lunette of St Benedict in the cloister of the Badia is described by Vasari (ii, pp. 513–4: 'Nella Badia della medesima città fece, sopra una porta del chiostro, un San Benedetto che accenna silenzio'). Milanesi (in Vasari, ii, p. 514 n.) and Paatz (i, pp. 287, 312) identify this fresco with an almost effaced half-length figure of St Benedict above a doorway in the cloister.

FLORENCE, San Barnaba. *The Crucifixion.*
A small fresco of *Christ on the Cross* is noted by Richa (vii, 1758, pp. 65–6) and Paatz (i, p. 325). This had disappeared before 1819.

FLORENCE, Certosa. *Three altarpieces.*
Three altarpieces painted by Angelico for the Certosa are described by Vasari (ii, pp. 506–7): 'Una delle prime opere che facesse questo buon Padre di pittura, fu nella Certosa di Firenze una tavola che fu posto nella maggior cappella del cardinale degli Acciajuoli, dentro la quale è una Nostra Donna col Figliuolo in braccio e con alcuni Angeli a' piedi, che suonano e cantano, molto belli; e dagli lati sono San Lorenzo, Santa Maria Maddalena, San Zanobi e San Benedetto; e nella predella sono, di figure piccole, storiette di que' Santi fatte con infinita diligenza. Nella crociera di detta cappella sono due altre tavole di mano del medesimo; in una è la Incoronazione di Nostra Donna, e nell'altra una Madonna con due Santi, fatta con azzurri oltramarini bellissimi.' Collobi-Ragghianti ('Domenico di Michelino', in *La Critica d'Arte*, xxxi, 1950, p. 369) identifies two damaged panels with *Saints Francis and Jerome* and *John the Baptist and Benedict* in the Certosa (panel: 142×70 cm. each) as parts of one of Angelico's lost altarpieces. These panels do not conform to the description given by Vasari, and are not by Angelico.

FLORENCE, Santa Maria Novella. *Frescoes.*
Frescoes by Angelico in Santa Maria Novella are noted in the *Libro di Antonio Billi* (p. 21: 'In Santa Maria Nouella tralle tre porte del tramezo, cioe del ponte, quando lui era giuanetto. Et in decta chiesa, doue loro tengono le reliquie, fecie piu ornamenti'). This description is elaborated by Vasari (ii, p. 507: 'Dipinse dopo, nel tramezzo di Santa Maria Novella, in fresco, accanto alla porta dirimpetto al coro, San Domenico, Santa Caterina da Siena, e San Pietro martire, ed alcune storiette piccole nella cappella della Incoronazione di Nostra Donna nel detto tramezzo'). This and other works in Santa Maria Novella are discussed by Paatz (iii, p. 836). The 'storiette piccole' seem to have formed the predella of a Daddesque altarpiece of the *Coronation of the Virgin* now in the Accademia (No. 3449).

FLORENCE, Santa Maria Novella. *Organ shutters.*
Two organ shutters with figures of the Annunciation are noted in

Vasari's life of Angelico (ii, p. 507: 'In tela fece, nei portelli che chiudevano l'organo vecchio, una Nunziata, che è oggi in convento di rimpetto alla porta del dormentorio da basso, fra l'un chiostro e l'altro').

FLORENCE, Santa Maria Novella. *Paschal Candle.*
A paschal candle (or casing) painted by Angelico is noted in Santa Maria Novella by Vasari (ii, p. 513: 'e in Santa Maria Novella, oltre alle cose dette, dipinse di storie piccole il cereo pasquale').

FLORENCE, Spedale degli Innocenti. *Madonna and Child.*
A small *Virgin and Child* owned by the Spedalingo of the Spedale degli Innocenti is listed by Vasari (ii, p. 512: 'Il molto reverendo Don Vincenzio Borghini, spedalingo degl'Innocenti, ha di mano di questo Padre una Nostra Donna piccola, bellissima').

FLORENCE, Casa Gondi. *Three paintings.*
Three paintings by Angelico are noted by Vasari (ii, p.512: 'e Bartolommeo Gondi, amatore di queste arti al pari di qualsivoglia altro gentiluomo, ha un quadro grande, un piccolo, ed una croce di mano del medesimo'). A. Venturi (in *L'Arte*, xii, 1909, p. 319) suggests that the Thyssen *Madonna* (see p. 201) may be identical with one of these three paintings.

FLORENCE, Palazzo Medici. *Five paintings.*
The following paintings by Angelico appear in the 1492 inventory of Lorenzo de' Medici (Muntz, *Les Collections des Médicis au XVe. Siècle*, 1888, pp. 60, 64, 85, 86):

(i) 'Uno tondo grande cholle chornicie atorno messe d'oro dipintovi la nostra Donna e el nostro Signore e e' Magi che vanno a offerire, di mano di fra Giovanni, f. 100.' This panel is perhaps identical with the tondo of *The Adoration of the Magi* in the National Gallery of Art at Washington (see pp. 203–4).

(ii) 'Uno tondo chon una Nostra Donna picchiolo, di mano di fra Giovanni, f. 5.'

(iii) 'Una tavoletta dipintovi il Nostro Signore morto chon molti santi che lo portano al sepolchro, di mano di fra Giovanni, f. 15.'

(iv) 'Uno colmo per uso di tavoletta d'altare lungho bra. 2 alto bra. 1½ corniciato e messo d'oro dipintovi dentro la storia de' magi di mano di fra Giovanni, f. 60.'

(v) 'Una tavoletta di legname di bra. 4 in circha, di mano di fra Giovanni, dipintovi piu storie di santi padri, f. 25.' This panel is identified by Longhi (pp. 173–4) with the well-known panel of the *Thebaid* in the Uffizi. While the entry in the Medici inventory perhaps refers to a picture of this subject, probability favours the view (advanced by Procacci, 'Gherardo Starnina', in *Rivista d'Arte*, xviii, 1936, p. 79, and reaffirmed by Salmi, 1950, pp. 78–9) that the Uffizi painting is by Starnina.

ROME, Santa Maria sopra Minerva. Two altarpieces.
Two paintings by Angelico in Santa Maria sopra Minerva are
listed by Vasari (ii, p. 516: 'Nella Minerva fece la tavola dell'altar
maggiore, ed una Nunziata, che ora è accanto alla cappella grande
appoggiata a un muro').

VATICAN, Cappella di San Niccolò. Frescoes.
The frescoes executed by Fra Angelico in the Cappella di San
Niccolò or Cappella del Sacramento in the Vatican are described
by Vasari (ii, pp. 516–7): 'Fece anco, per il detto papa (Niccolò V),
la cappella del Sagramento in palazzo, che fu poi rovinata da Paulo
III per dirizzarvi le scale: nella quale opera, che era eccellente, in
quella maniera sua aveva lavorato in fresco alcune storie della vita
di Gesù Cristo, e fattovi molti retratti di naturale di persone
segnalate di que' tempi; i quali per avventura sarebbono oggi
perduti, se il Giovio non avesse fattone ricavar questi per il suo museo:
papa Niccola V; Federigo imperatore, che in quel tempo venne in
Italia; Frate Antonino, che fu poi arcivescovo di Firenze; il
Biondo da Furlì, e Ferrante di Aragona.'
A further reference to the frescoes occurs in the *Codice Maglia-*
bechiano (p. 127): 'Et a riscontro di detta cappella (Sistina) v'era
una cappelletta; che si diceua la cappella di papa Nichola, ch'era
tutta dipinta di mano di fra Giouannj Fiorentino, frate dell'ordine
di San Marcho di Firenze, ch' era veramente un paradiso, con
tanta gratia et honesta erano dipinte dette fiure. Come anchora
qualche parte, che venne restata, si puo uedere, che ne tempi di
papa Pagolo s'e rouinata la maggiore parte per fare quella
sala grande che e innanzi alla chappella di Michele Agnolo.'

There is no documentary evidence of the date of the frescoes.
The now demolished Cappella di San Niccolò (which lay on the
opposite side of the Scala Regia to the Sistine Chapel) appears to
have been founded by Nicholas III, and was rebuilt and re-
decorated by Eugenius IV in or after 1433–4. Since Angelico, as
indicated by a document of 9 May 1447, had been working in
Saint Peter's seven days after the election of Pope Nicholas V, the
commission for the frescoes in the chapel of San Niccolò may (as
assumed by Pastor, *Geschichte der Päpste*, i, 1886, p, 270, and Beissel,
p. 89) have been due to Eugenius IV. It is, however, argued with
considerable force by Egger ('Capella Sancti Nicolai (Cappella del
SS. Sacramento)' in Ehrle and Egger, *Der Vaticanische Palast in*
seiner Entwicklung bis zur Mitte des XV. Jahrhunderts, 1935, pp.
133–5) that the presence in the frescoes of a portrait of the Emperor
Frederick III presupposes a dating after the Emperor's visit to
Rome of 9–24 March 1452. The portrait of Ferrante of Aragon was
perhaps included at the instance of Calixtus III (elected 8 April
1455), and affords an argument in favour of the view that the
frescoes were completed by assistants after the death of Fra
Angelico on 18 March of that year. If Vasari's indications are correct, the frescoes must thus have dated from Fra Angelico's last
years. It is suggested by Egger (loc. cit.) that traces of the frescoes
may survive on the former north wall of the chapel.
A drawing in the Louvre (His de la Salle No. 47), given by
Berenson (*The Drawings of the Florentine Painters*, ii, 1938, p. 245,
No. 1752) to Domenico di Michelino and containing on the *recto*
a study for a composition of *The Calling of Saints Peter and Andrew*,
is perhaps connected with these frescoes.

SOURCES OF PHOTOGRAPHS

INDEX OF PAINTINGS
BY OR ASCRIBED TO FRA ANGELICO